I Married a
Travel
Junkie

Mark—

It hasn't been 50 years yet (met in 67), but it has been a long time—

Happy Christmas!

Dad

I Married a Travel Junkie

SAMUEL JAY KEYSER

GEMMA

BOSTON

For Mark, a gift to you from your father and my friend of half a century. + with warmest regards,

Samuel Jay Keyser

20 Dec. 2011

First published by GemmaMedia in 2012.

GemmaMedia
230 Commercial Street
Boston, MA 02109 USA

www.gemmamedia.com

Printed in the United States of America

16   15   14   13   12   1   2   3   4   5

978-1-934848-43-2

Library of Congress Cataloging-in-Publication Data

Keyser, Samuel Jay, 1935–
  I married a travel junkie / Samuel Jay Keyser.
    p. cm.
  ISBN 978-1-934848-43-2 (pbk.)
  1. Voyages and travels.   2. International travel.   3. Keyser,
Samuel Jay, 1935—Travel.   I. Title.
  G151.K49 2012
  910.92—dc23   2011031540

Photo credits:
Photos courtesy of Nancy D. Kelly, Barbara Price,
Abraham Keyser, and the Author

... et eunt homines mirari alta montium
et ingentes fluctus maris et latissimos lapsus
fluminum et Oceani ambitum et gyros siderum et
relinquunt se ipsos nec mirantur.

... people travel to marvel at the mountains, seas,
rivers and stars; and they pass right by themselves
without astonishment.

CONTENTS

PREFACE

An excerpt in the *Gorilla Journal* dated June 18, 1999 begins:

> **Tourist Killings in Buhoma.** About 100 armed men entered Uganda from the Democratic Republic of Congo on March 1st to raid 3 tourist camps in Buhoma, Bwindi Impenetrable National Park. Buildings were looted and set on fire, vehicles were burnt, and 17 people were kidnapped and taken into the forest...the kidnappers hacked 8 tourists to death with machetes.

I read this article a week after returning from that very spot. Nancy had taken me there to look for gorillas. The year was 2007, our latest visit to Africa. It won't, I'm certain, be our last.

"Why didn't you tell me about this?" I demanded, waving the article in front of her nose.

"What would your reaction have been?" she countered.

Nancy always answers a question with a question when she doesn't want to answer a question.

"Jesus, Nancy. We stayed at the same tourist camp, in the same huts those poor bastards were in. If I'd known about this, I wouldn't have come anywhere near the place."

"See," she said calmly. "And look what you would have missed. If you knew about it, you would have been miserable with worry the whole time we were there."

"In other words what I didn't know wouldn't hurt me. That's your excuse for withholding critical information?"

"Exactly."

Being married to a strong-minded, travel-committed woman can be a real trial, or travail. "Travel" and "travail" are originally the same word with the meaning, according to the Oxford English Dictionary, "bodily or mental labour or toil, especially of a painful or oppressive nature; exertion; trouble; hardship; suffering." That just about sums it up. My wife's travel is my travail. In the course of our 19-year relationship (ten of them married), I have become, in spite of myself, what most people would consider a world traveler. This is not out of choice. My world-traveler status is an epiphenomenon— the cost of being married to Nancy.

Nancy and I were married on September 8, 2001, just three days before 9/11. We had planned a honeymoon in Bali. Our plane was to leave that weekend. Of course, the plane never took off. As a kind of consolation, a friend sent us a videotape of the ceremony. In it you could hear me reciting the wedding vows I had written. They ended: Whither thou goest I go. That was Ruth's promise to Naomi. I added it as an acknowledgement that I was aware of my bride-to-be's travel penchant.

But really I had no idea travel played so central a role in Nancy's life. I knew she had been to a number of exotic places, trekking in the Himalayas, spending time on an ashram in

Ahmednagar, India, climbing through the clouds to Machu Picchu, illegally crossing the Koshi River into Nepal, riding horseback from Lake Yellowstone to its source, Yount's Peak, the most remote area in the lower 48 states. None of that sunk in. Marriage was something you did to "settle down." And especially because it was a second marriage for both of us, I assumed Nancy and I would organize ourselves around the hearth, not the Earth. It never registered that marrying me would have no more effect on her travel itch than yelling "Boo!" has on the hiccups. I found that out the hard way, after two idyllic summers.

We had rented a house in Westport, Massachusetts, a lovely spot where farmland meets the sea. The house, owned by the great, great grandson of President James Garfield, was set well back from the road. It was a comfortable, single-storied, sprawling kind of house. It felt like a lanky farmer who had settled into an overstuffed easy chair after a hard day in the fields, his legs spread, his arms dangling. I loved that house. Every morning a herd of cows meandered by on their way to a meadow and every night they meandered back. In the interval between their coming and going, I would write and read and practice the trombone. One day I practiced outside. The cows stopped meandering, turned in their tracks and actually came up to the wooden fence surrounding the property. They hung their heads over the top rail. They were listening intently. I practiced longer that day. They seemed to like my playing. I was flattered. Great bunch of cows, I thought. Later I learned that the farmer regularly used a horn to call them to milking. They weren't entranced. They were just confused.

Somewhere during our third winter Nancy and I drove down to the area where we had spent those idyllic summers. The plan was to look for a place of our own. We found a real estate dealer whom we both liked. She prepared lists. She gave us plenty of time to talk among ourselves. I was certain that, sooner or later, she would show us the "right" place. I was wrong. No matter what we saw Nancy always found something that wasn't quite right. It was on the long drive back home one night that the truth emerged.

"I don't want to buy a house in Westport," she said.

"I thought you did. We had such a terrific time there."

"I know," she said disconsolately.

"You told me it was your favorite place."

"I know," she said in the same tone of voice.

"Well, then, what's wrong with our buying a house in Westport?"

"We'd have to go there every summer. It would make a prisoner of me. I'd hate it."

"No, you wouldn't," I replied. "Think about last summer."

She was silent for a long moment. Then she turned to me and said, "This summer I'm going to Bali and Indonesia. You don't have to come if you don't want to. But I can't spend another summer here."

She fought back tears when she said it. I think she knew that this was a critical moment in our relationship. Really she was saying, "If you want to be my partner, then accept who I am. Don't try to change me."

Those Westport summers were among the happiest of my life. Unhappily, happiness—like an open bottle of wine—is short-lived. Sitting silently next to me, Nancy reminded me of the woman in that classic James Thurber cartoon. A husband is sitting across from his wife. She is on the sofa holding her hands to her forehead and looking as if she were about to snap. He is saying, "With you I have known peace, Lida, and now you say you're going crazy."

I didn't say a word all the way home. I knew what was at stake. I had no trouble accepting who she was. Sure she could travel if she wanted to. A house in Westport wasn't that big a deal. So what was my problem? I was like a piece of old newspaper lying on the street when a semi drives by. I was caught up in Nancy's slipstream.

That was 21 years ago. Sad to say, we've never been back to my house by the sea. That is not to say that we haven't been anywhere. Quite the contrary. Since we abandoned the Westport house, we have been to over 47 countries, everywhere from Bali to Bhutan, from Austria to Easter Island. It has been an interesting life. I have seen cultures more at peace with themselves than my own. I have learned something about the thin edge on which so-called civilization is balanced. But all that has come with a cost. When Nancy declared that she couldn't stand another summer at home, my travel phobia, latent for most of my life, sprang fully clothed from my brow like Athena from Zeus'. I followed her around the world, becoming more and more anxious by the mile.

When she traveled, I followed along like the train on a wedding dress. I asked myself, "How could I do otherwise?" Think of all those sentences that might have begun "Remember the time when we...." that she would have to end up swallowing. I told myself many times that I couldn't do that to someone I love, that I had to suck it up and go along for the ride. But I didn't believe that for a second. Something else was going on, something that took me a long time before I could look it in the eye. So this is not a story about how travel destroyed my marriage, but how, as in any marriage, the effort to accept the differences between us was as much an arduous exercise in self-knowledge as it was in acceptance and empathy.

CHAPTER 1

~≈€ ❧≈~

The Journey Starts

Laotian monks taking alms on Sakkaline Road,
Luang Prabang, at 6:30 AM.

I remember the day as if it were yesterday, the day I first followed Nancy half way around the world. It was July 22, 1994. I had been 59 years old for just 15 days. Now my significant other was dragging me along with her to Bali. That isn't fair. She was going. I was dragging myself. The fact is I didn't have the courage, the strength, the objectivity, the disinterest, the insight, the-whatever to stay behind waiting for her to return. This was to be our first trip together. I mean first real trip, a trip that was not 200 miles away, like to New York City, but 10,000 miles away. We couldn't be going farther away from my comfort zone.

I've read that major life events like moving to a new house or having a child or losing a job can make or break a relationship. This was one of those make or break experiences. Anticipating the trip built an anxiety in me that came from someplace I didn't have access to. Never mind. Nancy and I were going to Singapore, then on to Bali, and finally to Jakarta and Djojakarta, Indonesia. Either that or she was going crazy.

As the days grew fewer until our departure, I receded deeper and deeper into the myth that we weren't really going anywhere. The night before had been devoted to packing. Nancy packed for me. It wasn't a mothering thing. She knew I didn't have a clue how to pack for a long trip. She, on the

3

other hand, was an expert. Still it took time. Long after my bags were neatly stacked and waiting downstairs for the taxi that would take us to Boston's Logan Airport for the flight first to New York and then to Singapore, she stood amid a sea of clothes, toiletries, cameras, batteries and the piles of flotsam and jetsam of long-distance travel. The floor of our bedroom looked like a yard sale after a high wind.

While Nancy was putting *Travel Smith* trousers together with T-shirts, I was doing everything in my power to make time stop.

"Would you mind going downstairs and bringing up those little mag-lights in the breakfront?" she asked.

No answer on my part. Just a loud clumping down the stairs, a yanking of the drawers open and a slamming of them shut, loud enough so that she would be sure to hear. Odd that. I was aware of what I was doing. But I was in the grip of resentment. I just couldn't stop acting like, well, an asshole.

I went to sleep a little after midnight on the morning of July 22. I knew Nancy would not get to bed at all. It seemed better for both of us if I were unconscious. The telephone woke me at 8 AM. Through the bedroom window I could see torrential rain. The wind was whipping the dogwood tree on our patio into a frenzy. George Whitehouse was on the phone. He and his wife, Gaby, were close friends. They also ran a travel business, CATS. It stood for *Custom African Travel Services*. I thought of it as *Calling All To Suffer*. They had arranged the trip.

"I think you guys ought to give some thought to renting

a car and driving straight to New York," George said on the other end. "The weather looks bad. Logan may cancel some flights."

It was as if someone had thrown me a lifeline.

"Thanks, George," I said. "I'll tell Nancy."

Maybe I'll be saved by the weather, I thought. Maybe we'll miss the flight and have to cancel the trip. "Who was that?" Nancy asked from the other room.

I wrestled with the thought of lying.

"Wrong number," I could hear myself saying.

Instead I told her George's advice.

"Nonsense," said Nancy. "We'll be fine."

She went on stuffing things into suitcases. That afternoon, through a driving rain, we took a taxi to the airport. The ride was excruciating, the conversation, painful.

"Did you remember to bring your passport?" she said trying to make small talk. She had reminded me a dozen times the previous evening.

"Umm," I muttered, staring out the window, but not seeing a thing.

I couldn't bring myself to look at her now that I was driving to my death, maybe worse. The plane would crash. The only thing I could take comfort in was getting enough to drink in me so that going down in flames would strike me as fun.

"Looks like the rain is letting up a bit. I've taken off in much worse weather."

"Umm," still looking out the window.

"They say Singapore Airlines is the world's best," she

chirped ignoring my bad behavior and talking on cheerfully as if I were right there beside her.

"Fuck Singapore Airlines," I said under my breath.

If Nancy heard me, she didn't let on. Rather she indulged me as if I were a child. I was certainly acting like one. I was caught in some kind of internal storm that was threatening to capsize me. I didn't want to be in this taxi hurtling toward my doom. I didn't want to see the Dieng Plateau, not at the risk of life and limb, my life and limb. A couple of Internet photographs in the comfort of our living room would have been fine, thank you very much. This was a mess of my own making. After all, it wasn't as if Nancy were forcing me to go. Who was I angry with? Myself, of course.

Our Boston flight was delayed a full hour on the runway because of the bad weather. I tried hard not to let my soaring spirits show. We arrived in New York with less than 15 minutes to make our connection. We had to get to the international terminal at the far end of the airport. I glanced at Nancy. I was about to say something like, "We might as well forget it," but the look on her face changed my mind.

What I had been harboring as my ace in the hole was threatening to turn against Nancy like a bad oyster.

Against every better-judgment bone in my body, I said to a cab driver, "I'll give you $20 if you can get us to the international terminal in 10 minutes."

It wasn't that I was such a nice guy. It was that Nancy was somewhere between panic and no-holds-barred depression. I had to do something. The taxi driver jumped curbs, went the wrong way down one-way ramps, passed other cars on the wrong side. He got us there in 9 minutes. I handed him a twenty-dollar bill. We ran as fast as we could to the gate. Our hearts sank. The waiting area was deserted. The door to the gangway was closed. A lone Singapore Airline employee stood behind the counter. He looked at our tickets and smiled.

"Relax. Bad weather. The plane is still at the gate. Your flight has been delayed for an hour."

He waved us through the doors. In a single gesture he had realized my worst fears and assuaged Nancy's.

Our flight to Singapore was uneventful. At least I think it was. I had two double vodka martinis and two bottles of red wine with dinner plus a scotch on the rocks afterwards. I was feeling so good when we landed that I didn't mind it a bit that our luggage was missing. Singapore Airlines said not to worry. They gave us a couple of travel kits, each with a blue kimono and a complete set of toiletries. They also gave us $75. This latter gift was especially generous since it wasn't their fault the baggage was delayed. I bought a pair of socks, a pair of silk drawers, and a blue T-shirt (I still have the drawers). Nancy did the same. Later when we flew from Bali to Jakarta, our luggage was lost again. Only this time we were advised to wait an hour for the next flight in. Our bags were on it. No toilet kit. No $75. Damn.

We spent 12 days in Bali. Our travel agent friends had secured the services of a driver for us. His name was Bantok. This was by Balinese standards an unusual name since everyone in Bali is called only one of four names—Wayan, Made,

Nyoman and Ketut. The names are allotted in that order. If you have five children, the fifth is Wayan again. And so it goes. Bantok means "soon, quick" in Balinese. According to Bantok, when he was born, his mother thought she had to go to the bathroom. She sat down on the john. Out came Bantok. Hence, the nickname.

Bantok was a godsend for us. He knew where the best temples were, where the best cremations were being held, where the best restaurants were, the best cheap hotels. He even discussed health issues involving Balinese women. Who would have thought we would be discussing endometriosis with our driver while weaving our way through rice terraces north of Ubud?

One of my favorite memories of Bali is a hotel Bantok took us to on the East Coast. It wasn't really a hotel. It was a thatched cottage built in the middle of a slew of rice paddies. We arrived late. It was almost 9 PM. We were hot and sweaty from a day on the road. We made for the hotel's outdoor swimming pool. Nancy and I were the only ones there. That's how I saw the Southern Cross for the first time, in a bathing suit floating on my back with my arms out, my body mimicking the constellation. That's when it hit me where I really was—halfway around the world.

In Ubud we had our very own valet and maid, Dewa and Dani. Dani would bring flowers to our rooms in the morning and place them on an altar outside the bedroom. She pressed her hands together in a prayer meant to bring nothing but good things to us and our cottage all day long. For each of the days we were there her prayers were answered. Every morning we would descend the outdoor stairway and take our seats in the breakfast room below our living quarters. Dani and Dewa served us black rice pudding, eggs, and tea for breakfast. At night we would order dinner from the Café Wayan, a mile away. There was no telephone in our room. We didn't have a cell phone, nor did Dewa and Dani. Everything seemed to work by word of mouth and motorbikes. Every night that we ate at the cottage, dinner came as if the kitchen were just downstairs. All of this for $45 a day.

"Are you still anxious about traveling?" Nancy asked me over dinner days later. I answered with a question.

"Are there poisonous spiders in Bali?"

It was not an idle question. We had arrived back at the cottage late that afternoon. When we stepped inside, I spotted an enormous spider, at least five inches across lying on the floor just in front of us.

"Oh, my god," I said, pointing to it. "Don't come in."

I rushed back out and ran to find Dani.

"Laba-laba," I said pointing up towards our rooms. It was the Balinese word for spider. I haven't a clue how I had come to know that.

Dani went upstairs ahead of me. She stepped into the room, picked up the spider and spread it out on her open palm, holding it for us to see.

"The spider was dead, for godssake," Nancy said with only the tiniest hint of exasperation.

"Yes, but it wasn't always dead," I replied. "One of these days we might not be so lucky."

The next morning I showered in our outdoor stall. The

walls came up to my shoulders. I had an unobstructed view of rice paddies below, the beautiful blue, cloud-smattered sky above, and, in the distance, the shrouded peak of Gunung Agung, the most sacred mountain in Bali. On its slopes was Besakih, the Balinese counterpart of St. Peter's in Rome. The shower was warm. The cool breeze that drifted across the veranda felt like Nancy was rubbing my back with her fingertips.

"This really isn't bad," I said to myself. "In fact, this is quite lovely."

That was when a bee stung me on my ass. I couldn't see it, of course. But it was a big bee.

After several more lovely days in Bali, marred only by pain whenever I sat down, Nancy and I left for the next leg of my maiden journey, Jakarta. Our plane landed around 6 AM on Sunday, July 31, 1994. As Nancy and I drove from the Soekarno-Hatta International Airport into Jakarta, I couldn't believe what I was seeing through the taxi window. People were asleep everywhere; under park benches, in the crooks of trees—Why didn't they fall out?—in doorways, on the side-walks, in alleyways. They were stick people stuck in the inter-stices of the city. I was used to seeing the homeless in America, but here was a several-orders-of-magnitude difference. What I was seeing for the first time, Nancy had seen countless times before in her pre-me wanderings. It didn't faze her. But I was totally unprepared. I felt myself growing numb, as if I had just taken a Novocain hit. I had never seen so many people in one place. It made New York's Fifth Avenue at noon seem like a Sunday suburb. Was I going to have to get out of the taxi and walk through that mob? How in the world would I manage it?

Our taxi stopped outside a high wooden wall surrounding the home of a friend. He was working for a year in Jakarta as an economic consultant to the central government. A gate in the wall opened as if we had tripped an electric eye. Our taxi slipped inside. A servant, a man, pushed the gate closed again, hurriedly, as if he were keeping the inhabitants of the street at bay. He must have been waiting for us. Another servant, a woman, came rushing up to take our bags (they were husband and wife). From the unsettling poverty of the city just outside those walls we stepped into a space of amazing tranquility. The living room was sparsely furnished save for a low table and divan. A water carrier that our friend, a collector, had recently acquired in Kalimantan stood on the low table. It was an object worthy of any museum in America, its warm, chocolate finish emitting a light all of its own as if it were a lamp.

The manservant disappeared with our luggage. His wife reappeared with tea and toast. We spoke quietly with our friends, planning how to spend the day together. The desolation of the city on the other side of those high wooden walls was now as far from my mind as America was from my body. I found this distance between the world I normally inhabit and the world of the people around me to be unnerving, disconcerting, surrealistic, even, as if we were in parallel universes.

Occasional reminders that the two universes were linked intruded. We were shown to our rooms. The bathroom was elegant, unlike so many of the bathrooms I had used since I had left home. It was equipped with a glassed in shower, tiled floors, gleaming surfaces. Over the toilet was a sign. Please do not flush fecal matter. Deposit it in the bags provided. The servants will dispose of it. Thank you.

Two days later we moved on to Djojakarta. As soon as we got there, we took a walk along a busy street. Every third step brought beggars pleading for money. I was not making matters any better by speaking to them.

"No thank you. Sorry! Can't stop. I'm late."

I found that very hard to do. It seemed so inhumane to ignore someone's plea for help. I soon learned that beggars were like multi-headed hydra. If I gave to one, two more appeared in his place. I was forced to adopt a suit of mental armor, bulling my way forward, staring ahead, acting like a robot. It was that Novocain hit again. I didn't like what it was doing to me. I have an American friend who refuses to travel for this very reason. He finds the great disparity in wealth between himself and the people in other countries too tough to deal with.

The beggars themselves know this. In Egypt street vendors offered me their products for nothing. They would insist. Of course I should have just said no.

"It is a gift. Please take it. It is free."

Then they would ask me for money. I would try to give back whatever they had given me. They refused. It was a matter of honor. I was a guest in their country.

"You must take it. It is bad to refuse a gift."

I learned to keep my hands in my pocket and keep walking. I didn't like it.

Sometimes the request for money came from the most unexpected places. In the Oriental Rug School in Egypt, the weavers are children. Our guide showed them off unselfconsciously, as if child labor were the most natural thing in the world. As he nudged us away from the workroom and into the showroom, the children, hard at work on their looms, would give me a knowing look and then furtively rub their thumbs and forefingers together.

It is a universal gesture, that: rubbing the thumb, the index, and middle fingers against one another. When made by children at a loom, it is easy to pretend not to understand. That was not the case at the Red Pyramid at Dahshur. I had stepped away from the group I was with. The pyramid's capstone had been removed from the top of the pyramid. It lay near the pyramid's base where it could easily be inspected. That was just what I was doing when a tourist policeman came up to me, pointed to the capstone, and then rubbed his fingers together just like the children in the Oriental Rug School. What service had he performed? He pointed out what I was already looking at. Even so, there was no way I wasn't going to fork over for a guy with a rifle on his shoulder.

Or take the workman in the tomb of Mereruka. Mereruka was a high priest in the court of Teti, founder of the 6th dynasty (2345 BC–2181 BC). He was the one who supervised the construction of Teti's pyramid, now pretty much a pile

Mounted tourist policeman at the base of the Red
Pyramid, Snefru, Dahshur, Egypt.

of rubble, all except for the burial chamber. The tomb is a
single-storied mastaba, an Arabic word meaning "flat bench."
Its walls are adorned with scenes of daily life. Strolling from
one room to the next is like skimming through the pages of
a 4,700-year-old almanac. The scenes are detailed, domestic.
On one wall, fishermen are depicted scaling fish. Below them
are the varieties of fish they catch. On another wall are tax
collectors. I was the last in line following our guide through
the rooms. A workman suddenly appeared from behind a
doorway and motioned me to come in. I felt privileged. He

had picked me out of the crowd, doubtless to see something special. He stuck a trowel in my hand, put cement on it, and showed me a niche in a column. He motioned for me to fill it in. When I did, he rubbed his fingers together. It was a variation of the free-gift gambit. I give him a buck. I think of him as an Egyptian Tom Sawyer.

The most inventive scheme I've ever encountered for getting a tourist to part with his money unfolded at Aswan, Egypt. We were in a felucca sailing along the Nile River to Kitchener's Island. We were headed for a walk through the island's botanical gardens. As we approached the dock, children in miniature dories paddled out into mid-channel until they came amidships of the felucca. They took hold of the gunnels, and while we were sailing along, they sang in a deeply Arabic accent "Row, row, row your boat, gently down the stream. Merrily, merrily, merrily, merrily. Life is but a dream." How could you not come across after that?

One develops certain defensive tactics but even these have consequences. Once our Vietnamese guide took us to Cai Be, an island in the middle of the Mekong River, to see how the locals made candy. Whenever we walked out of a shop or candy factory, a cloud of young children descended on us, selling postcards. I asked Nancy to buy a package so that we could defend ourselves against the others. One little girl—she couldn't have been more than seven years old—came up to me. I showed her my postcards. She gave me a look of disdain that took me at least 30 years to acquire.

The gift-giving ploy followed by the request for money must be nearly universal. It happened to me in October of

2004 in Luang Prabang, Laos. On our last day Nancy and I were up before dawn to watch the march of the monks down Sakkaline Road. The streets were empty of vehicles though an occasional tok-tok puttered by. In the distance a saffron dot appeared. It grew larger and longer by the minute, expanding as monks from temples along the route folded themselves into the line like floats in a parade.

Along the sidewalk Laotian women of all ages had put down mats and were squatting in the honorific pose, feet out to one side and pointed away from the monk as a sign of respect. They opened large rice baskets and scooped tiny balls of it, ready to be transferred into the begging bowls of the monks as they passed silently by. The monks moved briskly.

At 6:30 AM, slowed down by a steady rain that had been falling all morning, they were within half a city block of us, a long, saffron line, bowls slung over their shoulders, a black umbrella over their heads. They ranged in age from the very old at the head of the column to a young boy bringing up the rear. He couldn't have been more than seven or eight years old. An old woman sitting on her haunches in the street outside our hotel transferred handfuls of rice from her own bowl into the bowl of each monk as he passed. Nancy ran up the street for a better picture-taking angle. I stood outside our hotel watching. Suddenly, two old women descended on me. They pushed little packets of rice wrapped in banana leaves and pinned with a sliver of wood into my hands. They motioned excitedly toward the monks as if it were my duty to fill each monk's bowl as he passed. I hopped to it, taking the packets of rice from them and transferring them to the monks. I thought: How nice that they are including me, a stranger, in their morning ritual. But once the monks had passed, the ladies held out their own hands demanding money. I didn't understand what was happening. A member of the hotel staff interceded. There was much chatter back and forth. The staff member informed me that I owed the ladies $3. I paid it.

I came away from these experiences with the realization that I was defenseless against the wiles of the baksheesh seekers. It didn't help that I began with a full load of guilt in my pack. What was $3 to me? But there was also that feeling of having been taken for a ride, a feeling that I came into court with clean hands and had been handed a bill of goods. Then I thought: How could I blame them? They were so damned poor. My friend's strategy, just say no to travel, seemed like a good solution.

It was certainly better than the one I concocted out of self-preservation in Indonesia. It worked like a charm, but it made me miserable precisely because it worked so well. In the countryside around Djojakarta I learned that most of the people believed that defects like blindness, madness, or muteness were a sign that the person possessing them should be avoided like the plague. Maybe they thought it was catching. One morning a crowd of marketplace beggars assailed me. I felt panicky and claustrophobic all in the same moment. Nancy and I were without a guide to run interference. The idea struck me out of the blue. I don't know how or why I thought of it. But in the midst of beggars, extending open palms, trying to shove trinkets into our hands, offering to show us the local back streets, I opened my mouth wide and with my index finger I kept jabbing the air toward my tongue. It worked. They stopped in their tracks, backed away, and disappeared into the crowd around us. Feigning being a mute had restored my equilibrium. It also injured my sense of dignity.

Dignity can go both ways. On one occasion, this in Hanoi, I came out of a water puppet theater and was approached by a young girl, maybe 11 years old. She was thin with scraggly hair and just the hint of a hair lip, a slight malformation that was enough to capture your attention. She offered me a package of postcards for $2. For some reason I decided to haggle. I don't know what got into me, but there it was. She looked shocked. I insisted.

"$1," I said.

She came back with $1.50. I shook my head and walked away. She ran after me, tugged at my sleeve.

"O.K. $1," she extended the package of postcards.

I gave her the $1 but refused to take the postcards. If she was shocked before, now she was irate.

"I take $1," she insisted. "You have to take postcards."

I took them. I didn't feel good about it. But I did feel good about her. There was something so self-possessed and straightforward in her manner. She gave selling postcards a dignity I never thought it could have.

My companions and I milled around waiting for the bus

to come for us. It started to rain. Everyone huddled beneath the marquee of the puppet theater to escape the downpour, the little girl included. When the bus came, I turned to her and smiled. I offered the postcards. She hesitated, then smiled back at me and accepted the gift.

CHAPTER 2

❧ ❧

The Main Event

Maasai warriors jumping in place at a wedding held
near Ndarakwai Ranch outside Arusha, Tanzania,
in Siha District, West Kilimanjaro.

Our 1994 trip to Bali was a warm up for the main event: Africa. It was the first of seven to the Dark Continent over a period of 12 years beginning in 1995. I thought of them as the safaris from hell. They began when, on the occasion of her 50th birthday, I gave Nancy $5,000 to go anywhere in the world. Actually, I had given her the gift six months ahead of time because I knew even then how much she loves the run-up to a journey. This would be a gift that would go on giving for half a year.

These were the early days of our relationship. I hadn't taken the full measure of Nancy, Super Traveler. I was sure she would choose Italy. Why would she not? That's where I wanted to go. Or France. For a time Nancy and I would fly to Paris on a Thursday, spend the weekend in the city and then, on Monday morning, go to l'Orangerie to see Monet's Les Nympheas. Early Monday morning was a good time. You could get a jump on the Japanese tourists and have the water lilies all to yourself for an hour. Then we would head for the airport and home. Now these were, in my book, trips worth taking. I made sure she knew that. But for Nancy these trips didn't really count. She prefers places where snakes dangle from trees—for example, the Engaruka Plain in Tanzanian Africa where we once went to look for pythons balled up like worn out tires in the upper reaches of acacia trees.

The gift was a form of payback. On my 60th birthday she threw me an incredibly elaborate surprise party. Over a hundred guests came. It must have cost her a small fortune in both time and money. She never told me how much.

She staged it in our favorite restaurant. To get me there she had arranged a convoluted cover story. We were to stop by to pick up some hors d'oeuvres on the way to a small dinner party with some friends. Since all this was to take place two days before my actual birthday, she was hoping I wouldn't twig. She even manufactured a story about how I had to bring my trombone because someone at the dinner party was learning to play the trumpet.

"If you played a bit with her to give her confidence, it would be so nice," Nancy lied.

"I don't want to play with beginners," I whined.

"It was just a thought," Nancy said.

I felt guilty. In the end I brought my horn along. It wouldn't have mattered. Nancy had already decided that if I left the horn behind, she would go back and get it once the party started. All this fuss was to make sure I would be able to play with the musicians she had invited.

Nancy had warned all the guests to be inside the restaurant by 5:15 PM. After that the door would be locked. If they couldn't make it by then, they were instructed to wait until 5:45 PM. It was timed like an *Ocean's Eleven* bank heist. We arrived at 5:30 PM, ostensibly to pick up the hors d'œuvres. There on the steps was a musician friend, Peter Bloom, pulling frantically on the unyielding door handle.

"Peter," I said. "What are you doing here?"

He was embarrassed. That seemed odd to me. He refused to look at Nancy. Also odd. I never put two-and-two together.

"The restaurant's closed for a private party," Nancy said coolly, pointing to a sign on the door. "We're just coming to pick up some takeout for a friend."

"Oh," said Peter, "I didn't know."

Peter's misery came to an end when someone opened the door. He slipped inside like a squirrel out of a have-a-heart trap. In the days leading up to the party I had swallowed all Nancy's subterfuges hook, line, and sinker. When I think back on it now, I am astonished that I did. She was sure I had cottoned on to the surprise. I hadn't. Even though it would have been obvious to the most casual observer that something was fishy. I'm not sure what this means about me. Perhaps that I really am not very attuned to the moment; more likely, that I really want to be surprised and was willing to overlook anything in order to get it.

When we stepped inside the restaurant, a hundred people had covered their own faces with a life-sized photocopy of a face attached to a throat swab. From behind the facsimile they yelled, "Surprise!" The photocopies, of course, were all of me. Nancy knew nothing would please me more.

That's why I offered her a trip anywhere in the world. Nancy chose Tanzania. I was horrified. Africa was the place where they had Ebola and black mambas and shistasomiasis. Crocodiles lived in Africa. I thought of them as elephantine alligators. They killed people. So did hippopotami and Cape buffalo to say nothing of lions and tigers and bears. Oh my!

"Are you sure you want to go to such a dangerous place?" I asked on more than one occasion.

"I've always wanted to go to Africa," she said. "I can't tell you how much your making it possible means to me."

"Nor I you," I said. I buried my resentment for the next six months as Nancy planned a trip to Tanzania. An avalanche of African trips would follow: Botswana, Kenya, Malawi, South Africa, Uganda, Zambia, Zimbabwe, one every year or so beginning in 1995. Now that I look back at them they formed a progression, beginning with a blood-drinking ceremony in Tanzania and ending with a search for mountain gorillas in Uganda 12 years later. They also formed a progression in me. In the end I think I learned as much about our marriage as I did about Africa.

If on that first Africa trip my anxiety grew to outrageous proportions, it had the opposite effect on Nancy. All the while I had known her, she had been a nail-biter. If her fingers were ugly ducklings at home, they turned into swans when she traveled. Whenever we went on a trip, a real trip, she stopped biting her fingernails. For the first month after we got back, her hands were gorgeous. Then the trip endorphins wore off. The ugly ducklings returned. It happened trip after trip. That more than anything else taught me to regard Nancy's travel mania as something more serious than a taste for, say, vanilla lattes.

The closest I've ever come to fathoming it was when I read *The Nomad*, the travel diaries of Isabelle Eberhardt. She was an exotic character. Born to Swiss aristocracy, she embraced Islam, fell in love with North Africa, and died in the Algerian desert in a flash flood at the age of 27. In her diary entry for New Year's Day 1900. Eberhardt, who had been away from Africa for over a year, voiced an intense desire to go back. The revelation, to my mind, was in how she put it. She voiced her longing in sartorial terms.

"Right now," she wrote, "I long for only one thing: to reclothe myself in that cherished personality, the real and true one, and to go back to Africa again."

The travel personality, the one that wears a new suit of clothes, Eberhardt yearned for to such an extent that she even changed her name to accommodate it. In Algeria she called herself Mahmoud Essadi and dressed like a man.

I saw Eberhardt as a comic-book character, mild-mannered in Europe, but the scourge of the desert in Algeria, a kind of female T.E. Lawrence. It was that change of costume that got me. Nancy is very much like that—mild-mannered at home, but once she steps out of the house bound for Africa, a woman transformed. Her clothes are unadulterated *Travel Smith*, a company whose catalogues seem to breed in our mailbox.

Nancy pores over these catalogues like a philatelist looking for the One Cent Magenta. They only add to my distress. The latest one, for example, advertises a plastic hood you can place over your head. It comes with a protruding canister. The model in the picture looks like a pig that has just checked into a hotel. The device is meant to provide good, clean oxygen in the event of a fire. The same catalogue advertises a wedge that you jam under the door of your hotel room. If a thief, rapist, or murderer opens the door while you are sleeping, an alarm goes off. Fat lot of good that will do. They hawk a special hammer for driving. Should your car go over a bridge, you will need it to break the glass so you can swim to the surface. A lady's handbag comes with a steel re-enforced strap so thieves can't cut it loose with a knife. The merchandisers share my view of travel as an enterprise fraught with danger. They bank on there being a lot more like me. Knowing I am not alone is cold comfort.

The reason why these catalogues came to roost in our mailbox is because Nancy is constantly buying what they sell. When she dresses for travel, she doesn't just dress—she techno-dresses. Her jackets are thinsulate; her boots are Ecco's, $150 a pair; her trousers multi-task. They zip off at the knees to become shorts. Her jackets have to be loaded with pockets to accommodate the myriad gadgets that go along with her cameras.

Then there are the drugs: Imodium for diarrhea, Ciprofloxin for heavyweight bacteria, anti-malaria tablets that you start taking a week before you go and end four weeks after you get back. These pills give me weird dreams, a common side effect. They induce paranoia, though in my case it's hard to tell if it's the pills or if it is just me. There are jet lag pills, ingested according to a rigid schedule from takeoff to landing as well as tablets that dissolve like Alka-Seltzer in a glass of water. These are meant to protect you before entering, as it says on the container, "a germ-infested environment." Best of all there are antihistamine tablets that put you to sleep so you won't have to think about the "germ-infested environment" you are about to enter. Unless she were an employee of the Center for Disease Control, why would Nancy ever knowingly enter a germ-infested environment? Beats me.

It is not enough that Nancy techno-dresses. She insists I techno-dress as well. I wear trousers with zippered pockets, shirts with flaps that vent in three places and have secret pockets. I have four different wide-brimmed travel hats, not because I am hard to please but because Nancy is. I have underwear that you can wash and dry in less than three hours. This, I admit, I like. I have been on three-week trips with only two pair of underwear. (Dare I go for one?) I have earphones that drown out the noise of airplane engines. I have inflated headrests and a little device that you hang around your neck that purifies the air you breathe. I have several flashlights and an $11 pocketknife that I keep forgetting to put in my non-carry-on luggage. So far, it has cost me $28 to retrieve it. I know, I know. But I get attached to things. I have a walkie-talkie and a bracelet on my wrist that says that, in the event of severe trauma, I'm not to be given Ciprofloxin, any sulfa drug, or an examination that requires intravenous dyes. Since Ciprofloxin is the drug of choice to fight anthrax, I'm defenseless against that peril.

Unlikely I'll ever need it, you say?

I have been warned while walking in the African bush not to touch the skulls of dead animals. Why? There's a good chance they are contaminated with anthrax. Now when I see a skull in the bush, I treat it as if it were someone at my front door asking if I'd been saved. If I weren't paranoid before, this has certainly done the trick.

Thanks to Nancy, I have all kinds of luggage, carry-on bags, duffle bags, and equipment bags. They are all, of course, on wheels. I have combination locks for my luggage and locks that airport employees can open with a special key. I have pouches that hang around my neck for important pieces of paper, like money. I have a special packing pouch that instructs me on how to fold my shirts, my pants, even a blazer, into a package the size of the Sunday *New York Times*. One thing I have learned. However much I have, it will never be enough.

Once just before leaving for Africa I received a telephone call from a woman in the film industry. She was in Los Angeles and wanted to talk to me about some music I had played on a film she was producing. She wanted to know how to get in touch with me in the coming weeks. I told her I was about to leave for Tanzania.

"Are you taking any blood along?" she asked.

"Other than my own, you mean?"

"Everyone in Hollywood does," she said in a tone of voice meant to convey that perhaps I was too dumb to travel.

Turned out, blood was plentiful in Tanzania. The trip began with a Maasai wedding. I am as much a cultural relativist as the next guy, but I found their practice of drinking the blood of a freshly killed barnyard animal hard to take. I observed it first on the Engaruka Plain in 1995. A couple we had been traveling with decided that they wanted to be married by a Maasai chieftain. Don't ask me why. It seemed like a good idea at the time. There were no papers to sign, no examinations to undergo. It wasn't even legal. Just a romantic gesture on the groom's part. He had proposed to his bride under an albizzia tree on Gibb's coffee farm on the slope of the Ngorongoro Crater. In fact, while he was outside proposing marriage, I was holed up in a dayroom on the same farm, sick with safari fever, wishing I had never heard of an albizzia tree.

At a Maasai wedding the author and Peter Jones, safari guide, share meat from a cow that had to be slaughtered out of sight of women.

As part of the wedding ceremony, a goat was to be slaughtered and roasted. Among other things, we would have a once-in-a-lifetime opportunity to watch Maasai warriors drink its blood. (What is it the valley girls said? Gag me with a spoon?) Of course, Nancy would photograph it. I had no desire to see a Maasai warrior kill a goat, let alone drink its blood. But there was no help for it. Whither thou goest, I go. In retrospect it was not a very smart thing for me to have put in my wedding vows. Wedding vows are non-rescindable, or rather, rescinding them is tantamount to divorce, something I had no intention of doing. When Nancy announced that she wasn't going to miss the killing of the goat, my heart sank. Her declaration meant that I, too, wasn't going to miss it, in both senses of the word "miss."

Maasai women were not allowed to witness the slaughter,

although this stricture did not apply to Nancy or the other women we were traveling with. As far as the Maasai were concerned, my companions weren't really women.

"Are you going to stand for that?" I asked Nancy after pointing it out to her. "I think you should boycott the goat killing."

"You're kidding, right?" she said.

I did not want to watch the goat die. On the other hand I was certainly going to participate in the wedding dinner. I may be a hypocrite, but I'm not stupid. Roasted goat sounded pretty good to me. So, in my typical, tortuous fashion, I decided that if I were going to eat the goat, the least I could do was punish myself for it. Nancy, on the other hand, was much more straightforward. For her there was no question but that she would watch the goat die. How else could she photograph it?

At the time of the killing we were camped on the edge of the Engaruka Plain beneath a cluster of acacia trees broad enough to give us shade against the relentless daytime sun. Five Maasai warriors were looking for an appropriate spot to kill the goat. It had to be far enough away from a bevy of young Maasai women who had come to watch the wedding. They didn't seem the slightest put out by the exclusion. I took their attitude to be something like: boys will be boys and, anyway, who wants to watch a stupid goat die?

The warriors chose a dry riverbed just behind our tents. Dressed in red shawls and carrying spears taller than they were, they led a goat to the place where the deed was to be done. Then they killed it.

The killing of the goat turned out to be far less traumatic than the idea of killing the goat. One warrior upended the animal, throwing it onto its side. He put his right knee on the goat's neck and held his right hand over the goat's nostrils. With his left hand he stroked the side of the goat as if he were calming it. The goat quickly suffocated, kicking spasmodically at first and then not at all. I was struck by how easy the passage seemed to be from the land of the living to wherever it ended up. Almost like breathing a sigh.

As soon as the goat was dead, the warrior took out a long sharp knife and carefully inserted it about three inches below the goat's throat, piercing its heart so that blood collected in the chest cavity. The warrior then set about carefully and methodically skinning the goat. He cut the hide from neck to genitals, folded it back on both sides and, using both his hands and the knife, separated the hide from the body. He was like a mother peeling off her child's snowsuit after a day playing outside.

Next the warrior completely disemboweled the goat. One warrior took its lower intestines in one hand and squeezed out the contents between the thumb and forefinger of the other. A second warrior took the half digested contents of the goat's stomach, laid them out like a pie shell on the ground and arrayed bits of kidney, liver, and heart on the greenish brown mat. The warriors then helped themselves to the raw meat as if they were enjoying hors d'oeuvres at a wedding reception, which, in fact, they were. One by one, the warriors knelt down at the hind end of the goat. Like lions lapping water from a stream, they drank the goat's blood. The loud slurping noises and the bits of gelatinous material that hung from their mouths as they raised their heads raised my gorge.

One Maasai warrior filled his cupped hands with blood and offered it to a companion who drank from the out-stretched hands. Another warrior, who had covered his hands with grease gleaned from the intestines of the goat, rubbed his body the way Nancy might have rubbed her own with Oil of Olay. The goat's bladder and lungs rolled about on the ground beside the carcass like translucent party balloons.

Nancy had managed to photograph the entire event. She had mastered, so she told me, the ability to take pictures and gag simultaneously. I had no camera to occupy my thoughts. So I was able to spend all my time gagging.

CHAPTER 3

❧ ❧

Process or Goal?

Heads (moai) at Ahu Akivi, Easter Island. These are
the only ones looking out over the ocean.

On that first trip to Africa in 1995 Nancy and I were at the Ngorongoro Crater in Tanzania. Looking into the world's largest caldera is an overwhelming experience. At 11 miles across and more than 2,000 feet to the crater floor, it is the largest natural corral on the face of the earth. From the rim one looks down onto a lake in the middle and an expanse of greenery that stretches out around it like a tarpaulin. Through my binoculars tiny dots turned out to be a huge herd of Cape buffalo, their black intensity punctuated by the white of the egrets perched on top of them. To the left of the buffalo were a handful of elephant, on the far side of the lake an army of pink flamingoes standing upright in the water.

The caldera is 7,356 feet above sea level, the collapsed cone of a gigantic volcano whose peak probably surpassed Kilimanjaro's 20,000-foot summit. If you could stand back, at least in your mind's eye, and project the Ngorongoro peak, it would rise several miles into the air.

Ngorongoro Crater is a metaphor for life. There is a way in and a way out. Both are one way. We were on our way in by 7 AM, an unpaved and rutted passage that could have been designed by the Marquis de Sade. The reason the road was unpaved was that to do otherwise would detract from the total African experience. This, at least was the view of Tanzania's version of the Greater Chamber of Commerce. Africa, they reasoned, is meant to be an adventure, a walk on the wild side. A paved road into the crater would be like climbing Mt. Everest on an escalator. Maybe so, but if you're over the retirement age, the echt African experience is hell on the bladder.

The crater floor is a bit like an enormous zoo. Over here flamingoes, over there wildebeest, over that way Cape buffalo. The hippo pool was filled with 120 tons of hippo flesh, roughly 15 of the monsters. On the banks on the far side were bunches of cattle egrets taking a rest from their usual occupation, which is to sit on the backs of hippos and pick off ticks. An oxpecker can glean as much as 89 tick grams a day from the back of a hippo. The egret can down a lot more than that.

The egrets have left their calling cards on more than one of their patrons. They are artists of the avian world, turning the back of a hippo into a Jackson Pollack canvas.

We spotted a cheetah lying in the low grass about a quarter of a mile away from the hippo pool. Its head was up, looking lazily in one direction, then another. Two Grant's gazelles romped about 100 feet away and a wildebeest, alone and unprotected, was off to the left. If the cheetah were hungry, none of these animals, the gazelles or the wildebeest, would stand a chance. The cheetah's initial burst of speed is up around 65 mph. Some have been clocked at 125 mph!

"Lunch," Nancy whispered nodding toward the gazelles.

"That's pretty blood thirsty," I said.

"Don't you want to see a cheetah kill?" bearing down on want, barely disguising her contempt.

Frankly, no. I didn't want to see a cheetah kill a gazelle. I suppose it has to happen, the great food chain of being and all that. But I sure as hell am not going to exult in it. I am a hypocrite, of course. Since I eat meat, why don't I belly up to an animal kill and take it like a man? Well, I can't. At home I can't even kill a lobster, though it is one of my favorite meals. Nancy is the executioner. I'm the eater. There it is again, the lioness and the lion. Whenever we have lobster for dinner, she reminds me of my frailty, as if I needed reminding. I never considered myself rational, just normal. Well, that's not completely fair. Usually, when we sit down to a lobster dinner, I will call her a lobster killer sotto voce. She has good hearing. That's when she attacks my hypocrisy.

Before our descent into Ngorongoro Crater we had seen a list of animals that read like the bill of lading on Noah's Ark. However, three of Africa's Big Five—the rhino, the elephant, the leopard, the lion, the Cape buffalo—had all eluded us. They are called the Big Five because in the 19th century Europeans hunted them. Being hunted they turned into hunters themselves. So far we had only seen two, the elephant and the Cape buffalo.

After lunch we added a rhino to the list. It was so far away that to my naked eyes it looked like a boulder. Our guide had the eyes of a fish eagle. Sure enough, it was a black rhino, the only kind inside the crater, one of just 18. Through binoculars I watched it move back and forth, munching away for the better part of half an hour. It's routine was to lower its head, eat, look up and around, eat some more. In fact, this is what

39

all the animals in the crater did: eat and look around, just like us.

It was the rainy season. Showers appeared regularly over the rim of the crater, announcing themselves early so that we had plenty of time to close the hatches on the vehicles and roll up our windows. Someone in another vehicle spotted lions. They radioed the news to us. We rushed over in time to watch five lionesses do essentially nothing while their seven cubs chewed on roots, tumbled over one another or annoyed their mothers enough to make them get up and move to another spot. By the end of the day we had managed to spot four of the Big Five. The leopard never showed up.

The ride out of the crater, a 2,100-foot climb with seven switchbacks, was everything the park planners would have wanted. The road was miserable and there were parts where, had the vehicle tipped to the left, we would have gone crashing down a thousand feet to the crater floor.

The crater at dusk is the picture of serenity. The shallow soda lake in the center reflects a Magritte sky so that, like a Magritte painting, you feel as if you are peering through the Earth to the sky on the other side of the world. One evening at dusk the sky was blue and lowering. In the distance a layer of dark cloud hovered close to the horizon and in the middle there was a sharp upward thrust of white that signaled the presence of Kilimanjaro hiding behind it.

Off to the east, beyond the crater's rim, was Olduvai Gorge with its record of the gradual emergence of us. I thought of the sorry state of mankind compared to the peacefulness of the

Cape Buffalo graze at the bottom of Ngorongoro Crater, Tanzania, a caldera formed from the eruption of a three-mile high volcano.

crater. If the crater could talk, it would have said something like, "You see! This is what could have been."

"Don't blame me," I would have replied. "I don't eat fruit."

A half year or so before going on safari, Nancy and I had occasion to meet with our guide, Peter Jones, for breakfast in Harvard Square. He told us that at least one person on each African trip comes down with a mysterious fever. It lasts about 24 hours and goes as quickly as it comes. He added that the fever normally strikes within the first three days of a safari. We were into our second week when we visited the Ngorongoro Crater. So fari, no fever.

That evening we had dinner at the Crater Lodge. We finished early, around 7 PM. It was still light as I walked back to my room, skipping gingerly past the zebras grazing on the lawn.

Nancy stayed behind for a moment. I opened the curtains. A beautiful bull elephant stood at the bottom of the grassy stretch that lay between our room and the rim of the crater beyond. The elephant was standing abreast of a sign that read:

PERSONS VENTURING
BEYOND THIS POINT
DO SO
AT THEIR OWN RISK

The bull was quietly pulling up bales of long grass, shaking them free of dirt and stuffing them into his mouth. Nancy had seen him, too, along with everyone else at the lodge. She burst into the room, camera in hand, and ordered me out of the window and onto the grassy patch 30 yards in front of the elephant. My back was to him.

She stood in the window with her camera, shouting orders.

"Move to the right. Now back. Back some more."

While Nancy was setting up her shot, I was acutely aware that a bull elephant was behind me. I was caught between a rock, Nancy, and a hard place, the elephant.

"Now hold up your right hand…a little higher. That's it."

I heard grass being uprooted. My lower back began to tense. I could feel the spot where I imagined a tusk would most likely enter. I was very anxious to see the inside of my room again. After an eternity Nancy snapped a picture. At the sound of the shutter I made a run for the open window. Nancy extended her hand and hauled me in.

That night I came down with safari fever.

All night long I slept fitfully, waking every hour or so after the strangest dreams. In one Peter Jones, our guide, was ordering me to sleep in a tree. It was an acacia tree like the one baboons sleep in. Peter warned me to watch out for a worm that attaches itself to the bottom of one's foot and burrows inside. I looked. There it was, clamped to the ball of my foot. I pried it off with a stick. Its head stayed behind. I tried to keep the head from disappearing inside my foot. I was trying hard when at 2 AM I woke—sweaty, feverish, my mind racing.

That night took a week to pass. In the morning I got up, felt woozy, tried to get back to bed, and, overtaken by nausea, threw up. Nancy tucked me in, put a cold rag on my forehead and left to find Peter. Peter said my symptoms were typical of the fever. He said we could stay at the Lodge until 11 AM. I sank back to sleep. At 10:30 AM Nancy woke me.

"We need to push on to Gibb's Farm," she said. "There you can get a day room and rest some more."

As I climbed into the Land Rover, I saw by everyone's faces that I looked bad. That made me feel worse.

At Gibb's Farm, a stopover en route to the Engaruka Plain, I felt weak as string. I collapsed into the day room bed. Nancy brought me a bowl of rice. I ate half and was out like a light. At 2:30 PM Nancy woke me again. She needed to know if I wanted to stay at Gibb's Farm for the night or push on to the Engaruka Plain. I told her I wanted to go to Arusha and catch a plane back to America. I was certain I had contracted a strain of Ebola, one that killed slowly. I told her I didn't want to die abroad. It was imperative I fly back that night. She left to find Peter. She returned with bad news. There was only one plane a week out of Arusha. It was the one we were scheduled to take three days later.

"Can you manage the four-hour ride to Engaruka?" she asked.

"I feel miserable," I whined.

She hesitated for a moment. Then she said, "I understand how you feel. You can stay here. They'll take good care of you."

"You won't stay with me?" I said incredulously.

She ignored my question. "Peter will arrange to take you to the airport in Arusha."

"When will that be?" I muttered more to myself than to her.

"Three days from now," she said.

I groaned.

"You'll be in excellent hands here," she said. "It's just safari fever. And I don't want to miss out on the Engaruka Plain."

I couldn't believe my ears. Here I was at death's door and my wife was telling me she had to go to the Engaruka Plain. Later, she told me that she knew I wasn't at death's door. In fact, I wasn't anywhere near his house. There was no way she was going to let my hysteria stand between her and the pythons of the Engaruka Plain. She was giving me a choice between dying alone or in company. Naturally, I chose company.

The drive to our Engaruka Plain campsite was agony for me. I was lying flat on the back seat of the land rover, unable to tell whether I was shaking from the fever or from the bumpy ride over a non-existent road. When we reached the camp, the cook miraculously produced a bowl of chicken soup. He sent it over to my tent. The next morning safari fever was history.

When I'm on safari with Nancy, I never let her out of my sight, except, of course, when we're on a game drive. She'll be standing on the seat in the back, her head poking up out of the top of the Land Cruiser taking photographs. I'll be in the front seat sound asleep, or at least dozing. But we are in the same vehicle. I couldn't possibly imagine her going off to watch animals while I climbed a mountain or, for that matter, did anything, pleasurable or not, on my own.

Of course being in the same vehicle doesn't say much. I've learned that it doesn't necessarily mean we are sharing an experience. There are two kinds of people in the world— process people and goal people. Nancy is a process person. Me, I'm goal oriented. (I'll tell you how I found out who was who a bit later.) If you are like me, a goal person with a travel phobia, then you want to get where you are going as fast as possible so as to be indoors and out of the line of fire. This can be real trouble if your travel companion is a processor.

The importance of this distinction crept up on me unawares, the way the flu does, or stomach cramps. Nancy and I had been traveling in a small car on the wrong side of Tasmania's tiny roads. I was doing the driving. I kept misjudging the width of the highway, constantly drifting leftward. Whenever I drove over the corrugated strip at the road's edge, the car would respond with an enormous roar. Nancy thought we were headed straight into a ditch. Each incident amplified her anxiety.

That in itself might not have been bad, just harrowing.

But Nancy, being a process person, was interested in seeing as much of the country as possible. Goal person that I am, I wanted to get to our lodgings as quickly as possible. I was like a field mouse dashing from burrow to burrow. Nancy was like a bee, buzzing from flower to flower.

We were on our way from Cradle Mountain in the north of Tasmania to Freycinet Peninsula in the south. It was a four-hour drive. When we reached Launceston, she suggested we make a detour to visit Cataract Gorge. I fought to hide my frustration. I was fixated on getting to Freycinet fast. It was still three hours away. I didn't want to see no stinking gorge. Nancy added insult to injury. She said she also wanted to stop at Sea World. It had the world's largest collection of seahorses. I didn't want to see no stinking seahorses. She had put two processes between my goal and me. I ran off the road and onto the corrugated strip. The car roared.

"Watch out," Nancy roared back.

I braked to a screeching halt. "You drive the goddamn car."

I got out, slammed the door, walked around to the passenger side and waited until she shifted behind the wheel.

Nancy skipped Cataract Gorge. We drove for two hours in complete silence. It was a bad two hours made worse by the guilt I felt for having scotched her plan to see the gorge. About an hour outside Launceston I asked her if she were still angry with me. No answer. I took that for a "yes."

About an hour after that I apologized for yelling at her.

"What pisses me off," she said. "Is that you come along on these trips, but you don't lift a finger to help me plan them."

"You're right," I said sheepishly. Then, more boldly, "I think I'm trying to punish you for going."

She shook her head. "Punish me! Why the hell don't you just stay home, then?"

Why, indeed? The question troubled me. I didn't have an answer. Instead, I apologized again for not helping. It was the wrong time to point out that she wouldn't trust me with those details anymore than she trusted me to drive safely in Tasmania. Instead, I promised to help in the future.

In retrospect if I had understood how important the division between a process and a goal person is, I might not have lost my temper. It might have given me enough perspective to say to myself, "Look. We're 10,000 miles from home. We're probably never coming back here again. For godssake, take 15 minutes out of your goddamn goal-oriented, phobia-driven headlong rush to get somewhere and see Cataract Gorge."

Even now, I regret I didn't say that. Such self-awareness might have helped me to see that if you are a process person like Nancy, you will have made a list of all the important venues on a particular trip, say each of the lesser known museums of London like the Fan Museum, or the Old Operating Theater Museum where you can see a ghastly collection of pre-anesthetic surgical instruments. Each venue will have to be ticked off, like a pilot's checklist. The process person will not rest until every box on her checklist has been filled in. A box with no tick is like a splinter under the fingernail.

If you are a process person, you will be obsessed not only with the points of interest, but with how you will get there and how you will get back. Subway, bus and streetcar schedules will be indispensable. Ditto city maps with detailed explanations of the street signs. All of them will need to be translated before the fact. Where you have lunch will be a big issue. You can't simply walk into a restaurant off the street. It has to have been mentioned in the *Eye Witness Travel Guide* or *Lonely Planet* or *Time Out* or some such reputable guidebook, and you will have compared one entry to the other, looked at the prices, worried about the rate of exchange, wondered if the location of the restaurant will fit neatly into the next offbeat museum on your list.

It is easy to see where a clash might come. The goal person will simply want to get some food in his stomach and get on with it. The process person will say, "Not so fast. This restaurant doesn't serve the local beer."

While it is important to know which type you are, it is not all that easy to find out. That takes a great deal of introspection or else some catastrophic air-clearing event. It might be helpful to recount how I discovered what kind of person I am. Nancy and I were visiting George and Gaby, our travel-planning friends, at their house on Cape Cod. It was New Year's Day. Nancy and Gaby decided to walk to the water's edge on the bay side of the Cape. It was 20°F outside. A New Year's Eve snowstorm had left four feet of snow on the ground. The wind was a steady 10 mph, gusting to 20 mph. Nancy, completely missing the irony of it all, insisted that I come along for the sake of my health. The thought of going out into all that wind and snow was appalling.

We started across the Audubon Bird Sanctuary toward the water. It was cold, but bearable. Earlier some sort of vehicle had traveled the dirt road we were following. Like Good King Wenceslas's page, we walked contentedly in its tracks. No sooner did we come out from behind the trees and onto the flat swathe of beach that surrounded the bay than the full brunt of the wind hit us. The wind chill factor had to be at least –10°F. After ten minutes of slogging through the wind and snow, Nancy and Gaby announced that they had had enough. They were going back up into the trees to get out of the wind.

"But you said we were going to walk to the water," I complained.

"The wind is too strong. We're going back."

"But you can't do that," I argued.

"Why not?" Nancy replied, stunned that I might think otherwise.

Why not, indeed! That is when it hit me that I was a goal-oriented person. There was no way I was going to come this far and then turn back not having reached the water's edge. In that same instant I realized how absurd that was. It was viciously cold. The wind was merciless, the snow unyielding. I didn't want to be out here in the first place, but once I was here, I was in the grip of a higher force, something or someone that said, "Go to the water's edge."

I trudged on through the snow. I found the raised wooden walkway that led over the marsh to the water. It was an ice-coated wooden ribbon. Bent over like an angle bracket,

I struggled to the end. When I reached it, I stared long and hard at the icy fringe that hemmed the bay water at my feet. The freezing temperature had woven clumps of sea grass into the ice. They resembled mutant insects caught in amber. The wind grew colder. It started to bite like a swarm of black flies. I turned around and headed for the same hillock that was sheltering Nancy and Gaby.

I remember that picture vividly, of looking hard at the water's frozen edge. It is etched into my memory. That memory marks a critical point in my life, the moment when I realized that I was a goal person and that not everyone was. It explained a lot.

I am constitutionally incapable of searching out every nook and cranny of the Internet for the best fare, the best hotel, the shortest layover, the best deal. All I want to do is get there and get it over with. I don't really care how I do it. One airline is as good as the next. The same with hotels. So what if I end up in a lousy hotel? I can always leave. Not so with Nancy. She is all over these details like one gorilla grooming another.

For Nancy travel is not a destination. It is a process. Each destination is just one more point on a line, and, as everyone knows, each line has an infinite number of points. Her paradise is my paradox, a never-ending process, like a film loop.

When Nancy plans a trip, she does it with the same methodical attention that a clotheshorse brings to a closet. First, she purchases guidebooks on the locale in question. (Our third floor bookshelf rivals the travel section of a good bookstore.) Then she locates fellow travelers who have been there. She asks them to annotate the guidebooks. This fellow travelers love to do. Why is a mystery to me. My mean-spirited thought is that misery loves company.

Nancy's guidebooks contain more marginalia than margin. *This is unavoidable but boring. If you don't see this, don't come back. The food is excellent, but the service is only a notch above what you'd expect at a decent cemetery.* Nancy underlines the annotated venues in red in the index. Then she adds her own venues. The index becomes the itinerary. Missing a venue is to her what missing a mass is to a devout Catholic.

Nancy has an uncanny ability for finding the cheapest possible airfares. There was once a TV game show called *Name That Tune.* The idea was for the contestants to compete against one another by naming a tune after hearing the fewest notes.

Nancy plays her own version: Beat that Fare.

"I can get you to Rome and back for $850," says a travel agent.

"$650," says another.

"$590," says a third.

"$523," says Nancy.

She once got to India and back for $700 when $1,200 was the best fare a travel agent could muster. The Braniff Airline clerk refused to believe the price tag on her ticket. Nancy had to show him how she got it.

The absolute highpoint of her low fare triumphs was a round trip airfare for the two of us. I can still remember the moment when she called me. I was driving home from a gig at 12:30 AM. I was on I-93 heading south toward Boston when my cell phone rang.

"You won't believe this," she said.

"Why are you still up?" I interrupted.

"Be quiet and listen," she said. Her voice was shaking. Suddenly, I became very afraid. Something terrible must have happened.

"What's going on?" I said. "Are you O.K.?"

"I've just booked airfare for us from Boston to Rome," I could hear her trembling through the speaker.

"How much?" I said. I knew that's what she wanted me to ask.

"$1 each!!!"

"I don't believe it."

Now it was my turn for my voice to shake.

"And," she paused dramatically, "It's business class!"

I don't think anyone in the annals of late-night, computer-manipulated, airfare-fishing expeditions can match that. If they have, I want to hear about it.

To this day Nancy still doesn't understand why the airlines did it. There was no promotion or anything like it. Just $1.00 roundtrip. We paid it. We got the tickets. We flew business class.

There was one glitch. My seat wouldn't recline. Apparently, the mechanism was jammed.

"It's O.K.," I said, prepared to sit upright for the next seven hours. "It's only costing me 50 cents."

Nancy wasn't having it. She called the stewardess who gave us seats that worked.

Nancy is ferociously protective of her processes. This is especially true when it comes to her photographs. After our first trip to Africa, she sent me a folder of her digital photographs. A streamlined version of Photoshop had come with a

52

new computer I had just purchased. It was a program neither of us knew. I spent one entire weekend teaching myself its rudiments. I wanted to surprise her with what could be done with digital photographs on a computer. I produced a miniature album, Photoshopically leveled, curved, contrasted, and saturated. I arranged each of the photographs on a page, along with titles in different fonts. I incorporated flowchart figures for artistic effect. All in all I spent 20 intensive weekend hours working on the project.

I showed her the finished product.

"What have you done to my photographs!" she screamed as if she were Little Bo Peep and I had sacrificed one of her sheep to Jehovah.

Here I had just spent 20 hours making a photo album for her benefit and all she could do was yell at me. If you were to ask her, she would tell you derisively that I had placed pictures of us riding camels in Kenya on a single page hanging down from the letters C, A, M, E, and L like beads on a string. I thought it was a nice touch. O.K. I'm not a graphic designer. Still in all, I had spent the whole weekend with those goddamn photographs.

I threw the Photoshop CD down on the table.

"Here, dammit. If you don't like what I did, then do it yourself."

It was both a challenge to her and an accidental stroke of genius on my part. When I gave Nancy that trip to Africa, a funny thing happened. She was taking pictures like they were going out of style. I, on the other hand, like an ostrich sticking its head in an inkwell, was writing a journal. In the words of the Ba'al Shem Tov, "Where a person's thoughts are, that is where he is." Each day I concentrated hard on what I would write about it. Before I knew it, the day was over. That was one less day I had to spend in Africa. Here's the funny thing. When we got home, Nancy read the journal. On every page she said something like, "Oh, I have a picture of that." Or "You know the part where you describe the Dorobo leaning forward as if he were walking into a head wind? I got that picture."

Sure enough Nancy had photographed practically everything I had written about. That was when it came to me. Leonard Woolf had bought Virginia a printing press. He was looking for a way to ward off her post-librum psychosis. Whenever she finished off a book, it threw her into such a blue funk that she wanted to finish herself off as well. Putting Virginia to work as a typesetter was a masterstroke. Woolf must have reasoned that the way to forestall Virginia's depression was to arrange it so that her novels never ended. The ploy kept her alive for 24 years after the publication of her first novel.

The downside of Nancy's addiction to travel is that, like an addict, she is in constant need of a travel fix. When she is not traveling, she feels terrible. She is literally a travel junkie. Whenever we came home from a trip, her bags would stay packed for weeks. Unpacking carried with it the inexorable message that the trip was really over. I thought: Woolf's gambit with Virginia might just work with Nancy. If I could get Nancy to focus on her photographs (pun intended), then with all those photographs and all those Photoshop-portunities

A Hanoi motor biker en route to market
with two live pigs.

(portmanteau intended), Nancy would be too busy to feel terrible. The trip would never end.

I suggested that we (that is, she) make a photo-journal. Saddled with having to wed my words to her pictures, her hands were full as soon as we got back from a trip. No more un-emptied luggage clogging up the bedroom. No more moping around the house waiting for the mail to come. No more compulsive trips to the luggage store. Photoshop and my journal could keep the trip from ending.

It worked like a charm. Not only were the bags unpacked in less than a day, but mountains of photographs were installed on her computer. Once after a two-week trip to Vietnam and up the Mekong River into Cambodia, she came home with

7,200 photographs. I calculated that she was snapping away at the rate of 400 pictures a day, 50 an hour, or 0.83 pictures a minute. In other words while we were in Southeast Asia, she had her right eye glued to the viewfinder on average once a minute. She looked through a camera the way I look through my eyeglasses. That's who Nancy is. She only sees a country when it has a frame around it.

On that trip I found real peace in the sound of those minute-by-minute clicks. Each shutter snap represented another moment of tranquility for her (and for me) when we got home. For several months she would be immersed in problems of photographic layout and text alignment, all the myriad details that go into making a photo-journal. I had Leonard Woolfed her.

Unfortunately, the strategy backfired, both on me and on Nancy. The journal turned out to be a popular item. We began to get invitations to host trips all over the world provided, of course, we produced a photo-journal for the travelers at the end. It was hard to say no. I felt like the Sorcerer's Apprentice. Brooms were everywhere. I didn't know how to turn them off.

One year Nancy planned three trips in one. We were away for almost six weeks. To me that was like a lifetime. First we went to Tahiti, the Tuamotos, the Marquesas and Easter Island. Then we flew to New Zealand for a week. Then, for dessert, we flew from Christchurch to Casablanca for two weeks in Morocco: from the land of 40 million sheep to the land of a million camels in one long, seemingly never-ending 13,000-mile journey. The route took us from Christchurch to Auckland to Papeete to New York City to Casablanca. All told, we were en route for 33 hours, 24 of them in the air.

I have to admit it wasn't all that bad. The Papeete-to-New York connection was a tight one, less than an hour. We reached Papeete at 9 PM. We rushed to the designated gate. When we got there, the attendant asked us to step aside. That threw me for a loop. Did I look like a terrorist? Had I inadvertently left an apple in my luggage? Was there something wrong with my passport? After what seemed like an interminable interval, the attendant returned.

"We are upgrading you to first class," she said.

"Why?" I blurted.

I was so on edge at not knowing what was going on, the question just shot out.

"Thank you very much," said Nancy graciously to the attendant and then more quietly to me, "Shut up."

I have never flown first class in my life. I will probably never fly it again. But let me tell you, I can see why people do it. It was like flying from Papeete to New York in a hotel room complete with a female valet who changed clothes every hour and did everything she could to make sure you arrived stuffed to the gills and drunk as a lord. She gave us pajamas and encouraged us to change into them for the remainder of the flight.

"Does she mean here?" I asked Nancy.

"I think you're meant to use the restroom," said Nancy. She was acting as if she flew first class on a regular basis.

All that was the good news. The bad news was that once we got home from Morocco, Nancy learned that the other two trips she had planned—one to Papua, New Guinea and one to Madagascar—had fallen through.

For my part I was ecstatic. I wouldn't have to slog through the highlands of Papua New Guinea in a rainstorm, wearing a poncho and all the mosquito repellant I could find. I wouldn't have to dodge lemurs in the rainforests of Madagascar. While Nancy was on the telephone mournfully explaining to someone that the trips had been cancelled, I was going round the house whispering, "Yes" and pumping the air like LaDainian Tomlinson after a touch down—out of earshot and sight, of course.

My elation was short-lived. With no trip in the offing Nancy was thrown back into suicidal mode, a la Virginia Woolf. Photoshop couldn't hack it. Her bags stayed packed. Even her photographs were not enough to shake off the gloom. Something had to be done. I wangled a trip up the Danube and the Rhine from Budapest to Amsterdam on a 103-foot-long, flat-bottomed boat called the *Swiss Pearl*. From my perspective a riverboat trip seemed ideal. What was the worst that could happen? The boat could sink. If it did, the river canals were so shallow we could walk to the top deck and hail a taxi.

Things returned to normal. We took the trip and buoyed by yet another destination, she managed to unpack her suitcases, go to work with Photoshop, and line up trips to Bhutan and Uganda for the following year.

I have come to terms with my goal-oriented personality, at least to some extent. Like a member of Alcoholics Anonymous, I have acknowledged that I have a problem. I try hard not to control the rhythm of our trips, not to get in the way of who Nancy is. It doesn't get any easier. As the years go by, travel seems to ratchet up in our family. A trip is cancelled. The ensuing anxiety causes two more to spring up in its place. Never mind. Each evening, when at long last we have managed to arrive at a safe haven, whether it is a lodge on the Freycinet Peninsula or a tent in the Kalihari Desert, I break out a bottle of vodka and a thimble full of Vermouth. Occasionally there is even ice I can trust. Cold or otherwise, it does wonders for my equilibrium.

CHAPTER 4

❦

The Elephant Torture

Jay Keyser, the author, Nancy Kelly, the instigator, and Michael,
the driver, sitting on Tatu, the matriarch of the herd
near Victoria Falls, Zimbabwe.

Africa's three most dangerous killers—the hippopotamus, the crocodile and the Cape buffalo—have something in common: they spend a lot of time in the water. The rub is that so, too, do villagers. They need the river to wash clothes, bathe, drink, and fish. That's when catastrophe is likely to strike. If, by some mischance, an African should get in between a river horse and its river, the easy-to-go-postal hippo will trample the interloper to death in a headlong dash toward the watery equivalent of its security blanket. The Cape buffalo will trample him to death as well, not because it is anxious. It is simply an ill-tempered brute. Both are vegans, by the way. The crocodile, on the other hand, will tear you apart, eat the parts of you it wants and cram the rest into an underwater tree root until it's hungry again, maybe in six months' time.

Tourists in Africa rarely run afoul of these creatures. Their guides are too savvy. That doesn't mean that if you are a tourist you are out of the woods. For the typical safari goer, the danger comes not from the animals your guides have arranged for you to avoid, but from the animals they have deliberately hooked you up with: for example, the camel.

In 1998 Nancy—and, therefore, I—went to Kenya. We were headed for Rumuruti, a campsite next to a rushing river and a ranch accommodating 350 camels. The owner—his name was Jasper Evans—was a great camel booster. One evening over a campfire and a bottle of scotch, he lectured a group of us on how superior the camel is to the horse. It is a beast of burden that also gives milk, more than a cow and with three times the Vitamin C content. It is marvelous transportation. It even kneels down so you can climb up on it. You can eat it. You can eat a horse, too. But a choice between a horse hair coat and a camel hair coat? No brainer.

"Horses can't measure up," Jasper had said in a world weary tone that suggested the world would never learn. "They are nowhere near as even-tempered and certainly not as hardy, and as for horsehair, that's for flagellants."

Their only fault, apparently, is their susceptibility to typanosomiasis. The parasite had reduced Jasper Evans' herd from 500 to 350 camels in little over a year.

I was invited to ride one of these versatile creatures into the campsite. I could just as easily have driven in, or walked in. But this way the local camel drivers were provided with work. Nancy was all for it. It was a new experience.

When we found them, the camels were sitting submissively along the roadside. The head camel driver gave us a demonstration on how to mount. The saddle on my camel consisted of a blue seat cushion with a foam rubber pad under it and two wooden posts, one fore and one aft. I was to straddle the saddle. Then I was to grab hold of the two saddle horns: the forward horn in my right hand, the rear one in my left. This would give me stability when the ship of the desert sailed.

The trick was in the straddling. Apun, my camel driver, gingerly edged my left ankle over the rear saddle horn. He inserted my boots into the stirrups. So far, so good. I was now astride a sitting camel, a second bump added to my dromedary's one. When everyone was properly seated and instructed on how to hang on to the fore and aft saddle horns, the caravan moved into second gear.

My camel's name was Kidogo. It means "little one" in Swahili. Apun poked Kidogo under the back legs. Kidogo straightened them. I lurched forward. He straightened his front legs. I lurched backwards. Now I was sitting atop a camel some eight feet above the ground. All that stood between me and the dusty road, aside from the camel, was a blue cushion and two saddle horns. Nancy's camel was behind us. It was chewing on something green. Drool oozed out of the sides of its wide, rubber-lipped mouth. It wasn't happy. Perhaps Kidogo's sudden movement startled him. He spat his green cud all over my back. As if he were waiting for that signal, Kidogo moved off. I held on for dear life, one hand in front, the other aft. Green slim penetrated my shirt. It collared my bare neck. I felt like Lawrence of Israel: miserable.

Badly in need of a shower and a change of clothes I was very anxious to get to camp as quickly as possible. Not so the camel drivers. They kept the animals walking at a slow, stately pace to keep us safe on our perches. The wide back of the camel and the elasticity of my crotch being badly matched, my thighs began to hurt like hell. I smelled the same. To make matters worse, every time the caravan stopped—which it often did—Kidogo sat down, throwing me forward and then backward as if I were riding the mechanical bull in Gilley's Bar. When we finally reached the camp, Apun worked my left leg back over the rear post horn. I tipped him, thanked him for the ride of a lifetime, and limped to my tent.

The camp was in a beautiful spot. The tents were interspersed among a stand of yellow fever trees. The Rumuruti River ran right by our campsite. Papyrus plants lined the bank. Out in the river I could hear the hippos snarling like a bunch of aggrieved stockholders.

For me the hardest part of camping are the logistics of one's toilet. This evening Nancy showered first. She always did. Never mind that I stank like a garbage bag. The rationale was that it takes her longer to dress. People had already begun to gather by the campfire to listen to Jasper talk about camels.

Showers in campsites are primitive affairs. They consist of telephone booth shaped canvas tents with a slit in front that zips up. The staff places them a few feet behind your sleeping tent for convenience sake and a certain amount of privacy. Inside each shower, between you and the inevitable puddle of mud underfoot, is a wooden rack. A canvas bucket with a showerhead at the bottom and a pull chain hangs overhead. The staff heats the water in a huge cauldron over a roaring wood fire. They carry it to your shower and fill the overhead bag with the help of a small stepladder. They do this just once. There are other chores awaiting them, like preparing the evening meal. You learn to make do with what you have.

After Nancy left for the campfire, I slipped into the shower, turned the water on and let it run down my back to wash off the caked remnants of the camel spittle. I carefully turned it off to conserve water. I lathered myself all over. I pulled the chain again. Nothing happened. I poked the bag. Still nothing. I tipped it this way and that. Not a drop. Thanks to Nancy, I had run out of water. By now everyone was at the campfire. Maybe the next shower down had some left over. Stark naked, I crept down to the shower behind tent number 3. A reluctant stream of ice-cold water dribbled through the showerhead. After a cupful's worth, it, too, gave out. I tiptoed down to tent number 2. Same story. Tent number 1 was too close to the campfire. I slinked back to my tent, dried myself, soap and all, got dressed and managed to get to the campfire in time to hear Jasper Evans telling everyone that once a camel he was riding drank 28 gallons of water after going without for one full week. I knew just how that camel felt.

Wide-back creatures are to be avoided like the plague, elephants especially. When Nancy invited me to go on an elephant ride as a birthday present, I should have had the good sense to just say no. A van from the elephant riding company picked us up at our hotel, the Victoria Falls Hotel in Zimbabwe. We drove out of town and into the bush, stopping at a clearing where an open-air pavilion made of brick stood. It sported a thatched roof a foot thick. It was 7:30 AM and still very cold. As a sop against the weather we were served hot tea and biscuits and invited to gather around a wood fire. Shadrack, the major domo, told us that the camp housed 12 elephants ranging in age from 12 to 22 years. He told us the elephants were orphans. Left behind when poachers killed their mothers, these animals were trained for this sort of thing when they were very young, maybe three or four years of age. These were the elephants we were meant to ride. Shadrack warned us not to try to dismount while our elephant was standing. I couldn't see why the warning was necessary. It would be the equivalent of dismounting from a second story window.

Like a circus parade in a small town, the elephants lumbered into view, their drivers astride their backs, legs tucked in behind their huge, floppy ears. The drivers had no canes in their hands. They did all their driving either whispering into the ears of these giants or else nudging them with their knees. I followed the creatures to a corral where I was told to get to know them. I fed them peanuts. I blew softly into their outstretched trunks. It all seemed quite tranquil. Then I was invited to climb up a metal ramp that brought me level with my elephant's back. I asked Michael, the driver, if there was a sideways seat I could sit on. Alas, he said, the last one had been given to a family of four. They had gone out ahead of us. Nancy and I would have to make do without a double saddle to sit on.

Memories of the camel ride flooded back. Nancy knew immediately what was on my mind.

"You don't have to go, you know. You can wait here for me."

It was my decision, of course. Nancy would certainly have understood if I had gotten off before the elephant train left the station. But, of course, there was no way I was going to do that. It meant that I would be left standing alone in the elephant corral watching the circus parade disappear into the trees just beyond. Then what would I do? Find a shady spot and read a book? I would be at my wits' end waiting for the train to return. It was an impossible situation. I'd be in pain no matter what I did. So I did what I always do. I got on the elephant.

My elephant's name was Tatu. She was the matriarch of the herd. Nancy got on first. No problem. Then it was my turn. As soon as I put my left leg over Tatu's back, the pain started. It was as if I had been strapped onto a rack. The torturer was slowly forcing me to do the splits.

I squirmed and shifted and pushed trying to find a comfortable position. A young bull elephant, not one of the camp's 12, suddenly emerged from the bush. Even if I wanted to dismount, I couldn't. The young bull squealed, flared his ears, and started toward us. The drivers shouted something at Shadrack. He grabbed a rifle, moved out in front of Tatu, and fired a shot into the air. The young bull stopped in its tracks. It shuffled a bit as if it couldn't decide whether to charge or stand its ground. Finally, it skulked off into the bush. Michael explained that the bull wanted to join the good life the others were enjoying, what with their special diets, their enclosed barns, their coddling. I asked Michael how the bull knew about the good life. He said that every morning they let their elephants roam free in the forest. They always come back. Michael says that while they are roaming, they talk to one another. That's when the young bull got wind of the sinecure the others had fallen into. The problem was that the young bull was too old to train. They had no choice but to drive him off.

By this time Tatu was well out of the corral and on the trail. I squeezed my thighs hard against the elephant's back. That raised me up a bit and provided relief. I couldn't hold the position for long. When I lowered myself back again, the pain returned, more intense than before. The inside of my thighs burned. I was unwilling to ask Michael to turn back. The other elephant riders who had come with us were having the time of their lives. Being the birthday boy, I had been given the lead elephant as a place of honor. If Tatu went back, they would all follow.

"We're halfway there," Nancy said at one point, turning to me. "How are you doing?"

"We may never have sex again," I said.

She didn't seem concerned.

CHAPTER 5

The Lion Torture

Lioness in South Luangwa River National Park, Zambia,
waiting for something to kill.

In an article in the *New Yorker* magazine of April 2007, Werner Herzog is quoted as saying, "I try to understand the ocean beneath the thin layer of ice that is civilization. There are miles and miles of Deep Ocean, of darkness and barbarism. And I know the ice can break easily." That's pretty much how I feel about traveling, especially when I am in places where the wild things are, like the African bush. I am afraid for my safety. I can't help focus on the very real possibility that there are things out there that will kill me. Nancy and her (my) traveling companions couldn't be more carefree. They are as optimistic as Master Pangloss, the preceptor who taught Voltaire's Candide that wherever we are is the best of all possible worlds or, in this instance, jungles. This difference in attitude is not surprising. My companions are, after all, where they want to be. I, on the other hand, am tiptoeing around the bush like a rabbit at an NRA convention. This wouldn't be worth mentioning were it not for the fact that a rose-colored attitude can have its disadvantages.

This was never more apparent than the time in 1999 when I was in Zambia at the South Luangwa River National Park. Only six of us were allowed to go on this particular walk for reasons of safety—six, that is, plus a guide, a scout armed with a .438 high powered rifle, hard-nosed and dum-dum bullets and a bearer, Robert, carrying tea, coffee and a Tupperware container of chocolate cake. The scout was named Godfrey. He worked for the National Parks and Wildlife Association of Zambia. The guide was Simon. He and Robert worked for Robin Pope Safaris.

Two days earlier another group of walkers had covered the same ground we were about to—a circle inside an oxbow of the South Luangwa River. The earlier group had spotted four lionesses and nine cubs crossing a clearing about 75 yards away from them. And now we were setting out at 6 AM to see if we could do the same. I mean, how crazy do you have to be before someone locks you up?

We reached the edge of the Luangwa River by mid-morning. The plan was to stop for tea under a huge acacia tree growing in a meadow above the river. Just to the right of the tree was an opening in a high bank. It led down to the water. We stepped into the meadow in time to see a massive hippo filling the opening. Even though his back was to us, he knew we were there. He was nervous about it. He tried to face us but couldn't turn around thanks to his huge bulk. Unable to back out, he had only one choice left. He took it. A few seconds later a mushroom cloud of dust rose up over the top of the bank. We walked to the opening. The drop from the top of the embankment to the water's edge was at least ten feet, a difficult jump for any of us. This 6,000-pound creature negotiated it with ease. By the time we had reached the opening, he was walking out toward the center of the river, safer in his element than we were in ours.

After tea, I looked at my watch. Only two more hours to go

before we were due back at camp. Robert packed up. Simon suggested we continue our search for the lions.

"Why, for godssake?" I wanted to shout.

I didn't, of course. Everyone would have hated me. I kept quiet and hoped against hope that the rest of the trek would be lion-less. The sun was hot and, having walked for three hours and four miles, I was tired, cranky, and, most of all, apprehensive. I didn't want to find lions. I just wanted to get back to the camp in one piece. Today it seemed as if the lions had gone fishing. Fine with me.

We came to a meadow. Gaby Whitehouse, an avid bird-watcher, spotted a battleur eagle and a vulture circling over a thicket 100 yards to our right.

"Let's see what's over there," she said.

We walked along a dusty service road. It took us straight to the thicket. Suddenly Simon pointed to the ground. A large red stain the color of burgundy had recently soaked into the newly softened earth. Next to it was an amorphous brown mound. To me it looked like dung. On a walking safari, one soon discovers that dung is everywhere. The ground is either dust or dung.

"This isn't dung," said Simon.

He kicked the mound open with his foot. It was the contents of an impala's stomach. The brown gave way to green and a swarm of tiny insects spurted up like a miniature geyser. The green was the grass the impala was eating just before it was killed. We walked a few yards further. There was a second kill, this one just like the first—a large red spot, the contents of a stomach. Simon was very alert now. I was beginning to get very nervous. I wanted out. Not my five companions. This stalking was like some kind of drug. The more they did, the more they wanted. This had turned into a kind of *folie à six* minus one.

We moved to the border of the thicket. It was on our left. We were skirting it slowly. Someone thought she heard something inside and signaled to Simon and Godfrey. To our right was a field of brown grass about two feet high. We were walking single file now, as instructed, and peering intently into the thicket on our left. Suddenly a roar that sounded as if it had traveled from somewhere deep inside the earth exploded over the meadow. I looked to my right. Four lionesses were standing in the grass under a tree 20 yards away. Nine cubs came bounding through the grass towards us. They looked as if they wanted to play.

I thought, "God! If they come over here, we are in for it."

I looked back at the lionesses. One of them had taken several steps in our direction, a mock charge. She stopped and roared again. Her tail was twitching. She pawed the ground. I learned later these were telltale signs that she was a hair trigger away from charging.

I knew there were four lionesses, but now I could only see three. I lost track of the cubs. I was very scared, but, surprisingly, I didn't panic. Simon raised his arms like a stork drying its wings.

"Move back," he commanded. "Move back. Keep moving back."

Godfrey stepped in front of us. His rifle was cocked. He was watching the dominant lioness, the one who had leapt out in front. I was dimly aware that Robert, the bearer, was on my left and that someone else was on my right. They both had hold of me. Why, I don't know. I hadn't tripped, faltered, or fainted. Maybe they needed someone to hang on to.

Robert kept repeating, "Don't run." I hadn't the slightest intention of running. There was no way I was going to out-run a lioness.

"Move back," said Simon, in counterpoint to Robert's "don't run."

I followed their orders to the letter, keeping my eyes on the lionesses but moving back steadily. I glanced over my left shoulder. Jesus Christ! A hippopotamus was behind us, maybe 30 yards away.

"Will they both attack at once," I wondered. "How many shots can Godfrey get off?"

"Psst," I whispered to Simon.

"What!" he sounded irritated.

"We can't keep moving back," I said.

"Why?" he snapped.

"There's a hippo behind us," cocking my head in its direction.

Simon saw the wisdom in my remark.

"Stop," he said and then, God knows why, "Move forward."

We did. The alpha female roared again. Then she charged, another mock charge, but this time I was sure it was all over. I looked at Nancy for what I was certain was the last time ever. She was just in front of me. For godssake, she was taking pictures. She turned and held out her hand for me to see. It was shaking like a leaf. Later she told me that when the lioness charged, she'd muttered, "Shit," followed immediately by the thought. "Oh, great. My last word on Earth will be 'shit.'" (I never understood why that mattered to her. It wasn't as if anyone were recording this fiasco for posterity.)

"Move to the left," ordered Simon.

Slowly, slowly, we sidled out from between the lionesses and the hippo, up a rise and away from the meadow. We found ourselves on the dried bottom of a lagoon, one of the many formed during the rainy season when the river overflowed. We followed it to the river. On a tree-filled knoll overlooking the water, the camp staff had set up lunch. It was meant to be a surprise. There were drinks. I had four gin and tonics in a row, one right after the other. That was the only time in my life I have ever binge drunk. It didn't help. I was sober as a judge. Back at camp, I crashed. I slept for two hours. Nancy, who had spent the afternoon taking pictures of hippos in the river, woke me in time to join her for the evening game drive. She is nothing if not thoughtful.

That night I was treated to an African bush Grand Guignol. I saw a dead impala hanging from the branches of a large tree, its snout pointing down like some kind of grotesque plumb line. A small leopard, a female, was in the tree gnawing inside the chest of the carcass. It had been ripped open exposing the rib cage. Two hyenas appeared below the carcass. Unlike leopard, they cannot climb trees. They kept leaping up, trying to snag the head. Just then in the bush to our right, another, larger leopard, a male, began slinking toward the tree. I thought he was stalking the hyena.

These animals were studies in focus. None of them had any interest in anything except the meat. The slinking leopard jumped into the tree and darted up the limb to the dangling impala. A snarling fight broke out. The male knocked the female out of the tree. In an amazing demonstration of athletic dexterity, she caught herself with her front paws just before she reached the jaws of the hyenas. She swung back and forth like a pendulum, holding on as long as she could. Finally, she lost her grip and crashed down onto the back of one of the hyenas. There was another fusillade of snarls and a thrashing of limbs. Once again the leopard somehow managed to escape. One of the hyenas followed her into the bush, but almost immediately gave up the chase. By the time he returned, the male leopard had settled down to the carcass. Then, surprisingly, after just a few bites, hardly enough to justify all that combat, he scampered back down the limb and disappeared. The hyenas continued to mill around beneath the carcass, like a couple of drunks unwilling to go home after the bar had closed. Every now and then, in Tantalus fashion, they jumped up. They kept missing the head by inches. To add insult to injury, the female leopard returned to the tree, took up her place by the carcass, and started eating again. We were back where it had started a quarter of an hour earlier, watching a female leopard alone in a tree munching on a dead gazelle.

Daud, our driver, said that in all his years as a guide, he had never seen two leopards fight. Our safari leaders said that in the 18 years of running African safaris they had never had an encounter like the one with the lions. It had been, they said, an extraordinary day.

Back at camp that evening, someone asked me if I had enjoyed myself. Here is what I thought. That morning I had had a near miss with a hippo, a brush with death in the guise of a quartet of lionesses. That evening I watched two leopards and two hyenas trying their level best to devour either one another or the mutilated carcass of a gazelle hanging in a tree, whichever came first. And for this I was paying good money.

As my mother used to say, somebody saw me coming.

I think this was the first time in my life that I have ever confronted real fear, not the fear that knots your stomach when you're a kid and you realize you are going to have to fight somebody because they called you "a son of a bitch." (In my neighborhood any slight against one's mother had to be avenged.) This was fear mixed with a healthy dose of anger. I had been telling my companions and the guides and Nancy that it was absolutely crazy to go looking for lions, especially on foot. What was the point? Everybody knows what a lion looks like. And when it is chest-high looking right back at you, there better be a bunch of bars in between. Why couldn't they see that? The more I complained, the more sympathetic their smiles. It was maddening.

"Jay is really a hoot, isn't he?" they would say patronizingly. "Afraid to go looking for lions. I'll bet he never goes out after 10 PM."

You're damned right, I don't. And I don't go looking for lions either. I've learned that in this world even if you stay put, trouble will find you. Where's the percentage in looking for it?

Looking back on it now, I am not surprised that I didn't panic. I read about a sailor who set out to circumnavigate the world single-handedly in a 26-foot boat. He decided to round Cape Horn the wrong way. On his first attempt a huge storm drove him several hundred miles back into the South Atlantic. He fought and fought and fought until, at one point, the seas simply overwhelmed him. He went below, battened down the hatch and waited to die. After a short while, the boat started to list. It didn't stop. In a few moments it was upside down in the water. He described his reaction. He stopped fighting. He was flooded with a sudden sense of ease. The fight was over. He didn't have anything left to do but let the ocean take him. Then, miraculously, the boat slowly righted itself. He was off and running again. For a few beatific moments bliss had been his.

That's how I felt when the lions roared. I had talked and talked and tried my best to get Nancy to abandon this foolishness. I knew she wouldn't and I knew I wouldn't leave her alone on the oxbow while I stayed back in camp drinking tea. So it came to this. The lions roared. And, instead of panic, I felt fear, anger, and then, just as suddenly, a sense of beatific ease. I can tell you exactly what it felt like. It felt the way you do just before a colonoscopy. The nurse injects something into your veins and instead of dreading the probe, you welcome it with a big, goofy smile on your face.

There was an aftermath. From then on I realized that an

unbreachable wall exists between Nancy and me. Despite everything we share, there is one thing we can never share. That is a sense of impending doom. In his book, *The Blank Slate*, Steven Pinker writes:

> If you have a longer than average version of the D4DR dopamine receptor gene, you are more likely to be a thrill seeker, the kind of person who jumps out of airplanes, clambers up frozen waterfalls, or has sex with strangers. If you have a shorter version of a stretch of DNA that inhibits the serotonin transporter gene on chromosome 17, you are more likely to be neurotic and anxious, the kind of person who can barely function at social gatherings for fear of offending someone or acting like a fool.

Now I know that Nancy and I live on different sides of that genetic fence. Her D4DR dopamine receptor gene must be as long as her arm, while mine is as short as a wasp's temper. She is a risk-taker par excellence. If there were an Olympics for risk-avoiders, I'd be a gold medalist. I tell her that putting oneself in harm's way is like playing golf on a firing range. She says, "Don't knock it if you haven't tried it."

My fear, of course, is paranoia, but it is not just paranoia. I was on a night game drive in Tanzania about 50 miles outside of Arusha. It was in January of 2004. We were staying at a lodge called Ndarakwai that belonged to Peter Jones. The drive had been filled with enough sightings to satisfy everyone. I was dozing from a long day and two shots of scotch before dinner. I was about as relaxed as I could ever get on safari when suddenly, caught in the headlights just in front of us, was an aardvark. This is an animal that Nancy and I had wanted to see ever since we started coming to Africa in 1995, Nancy, because it was so hard to find, being completely nocturnal and extraordinarily shy and I, because I play second trombone in the Aardvark Jazz Orchestra in Boston. I wanted to be able to go home and tell my fellow band members that I'd actually seen the orchestra's avatar.

At first everyone was thrilled to see the animal dart around as if it were trying to get out of the spotlight, something it couldn't possibly do. It was far too big for that. A typical aardvark weighs at least 150 pounds. This one looked a lot sturdier. It had a high rounded body and a narrow head with ears that stuck out on either side like wafer-shaped ice cream cones. Its nose was long and came to a blunt point. Its forelegs were short and its claws made Edward Scissorhands look like a nail-biter. I was especially interested in those claws. They were powerful enough to dig a five-foot deep hole in the savannah floor in as many minutes.

Things can go sour quickly on safari. In an instant what had been an incredible sighting of a difficult to come by animal turned into something far more ominous. I was sitting in the passenger seat of the Land Cruiser, an open vehicle without a roof or sides. Only three and a half feet and a low-slung door separated me from the ground. The aardvark started to run around like a chicken with its head cut off. It headed into the bush. If it had had any sense, it would have kept going. Suddenly it wheeled around and ran head on into the Land Cruiser right where I was sitting. Nothing but the low door separated it from me. It bounced off with a loud bonk. I felt the impact against my leg.

"That must really hurt," I thought.

Apparently not. It spun around, and rammed the door again and again. It tried twice to get underneath the vehicle, probably trying to upend it, but we were too low to the ground and it was too big.

Things were now at the point where it would have endangered the animal were the Land Cruiser to move. Not that I would have minded that much. But the women behind me were beside themselves with concern for the creature. I was, for all intents and purposes, chopped liver.

"We might run over it," said one of them while I was trying to gauge how high the damn thing could jump.

One slash from those powerful forearms and my forearm would literally have been chopped liver. Our driver—he had the unlikely name of Telex—was chuckling like a Frenchman at a Jerry Lewis movie. The aardvark took another run at the Land Cruiser and/or me. It was as if the vehicle were the bell at Notre Dame Cathedral and the aardvark, its clapper.

"Turn off the light," the women implored.

Telex reluctantly complied. This was a first for him—an aardvark in attack mode. The sudden darkness did it. Perhaps the animal thought it had killed us when the light went out. In any event it took off up the road and its plump, rounded rear, now illuminated only by our parking lights, disappeared into the bush.

Back at Ndarakwai we told the story to Peter Jones. He said he had never heard of an aardvark behaving like that.

Everyone speculated. Did the light blind it? Confuse it? Enrage it? Maybe it was rabid. Was it just trying to get out the way it had come in, only a Land Cruiser was blocking the exit? We are all supposed to learn from our experience. What did I learn? Next time sit in the back.

CHAPTER 6

New Cramps for Old

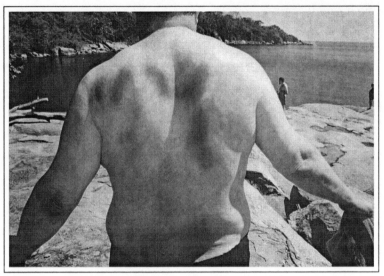

The author's scratched and bleeding back and elbows after being
hauled out of shistosomiasis infested Lake Malawi.

Bilharzias disease is carried by a tiny wormlike parasite that lives in Lake Malawi, the lake we were going to snorkel in the summer of 1998. Lake Malawi has more species of fish than any other lake in the world, over 600 endemic species. The snorkelers among us were anxious to catch a glimpse of the fish. I was anxious about catching bilharzias. This was not the only time our anxieties were 180° out of phase.

The bilharzias parasite thrives in fecal matter deposited into Lake Malawi from non-sanitary village discharges along its perimeter. It enters the body through the skin, boring like a miniature awl. Once inside it migrates to whatever system pleases it. There it propagates until the system breaks down, producing paralysis, blindness, or worse. We were assured that every precaution had been taken.

For one thing we were not going to snorkel offshore. We were going to take a motorboat way out to an uninhabited island, far from the fecal matter. For a second, as soon as we were out of the water we were instructed to towel off immediately since the parasite is transferred from lake to skin through tiny droplets of water. For a third, we were to rub ourselves all over with alcohol. That would kill whatever parasites managed to escape the toweling.

At Lake Malawi's Monkey Bay, we gathered our snorkeling and scuba gear and got into the boat that took us to the island. The trip was a quick one. Not quick enough to keep water from seeping in at a great rate. By the time we arrived I was sitting in three inches of Lake Malawi and lord knows how many parasites without having stepped out of the boat.

I had never snorkeled before. Everyone assured me it was a piece of cake. I put the flippers and the mask on and slipped off the rocky shoreline of the island into the water. The drop was steep, not gradual, as I had expected. As soon as I entered the water, it was over my head. Suddenly I had to think about the mask, the breathing tube, the flippers and keeping afloat, all at the same time. This was too much for me. Nancy was standing on a submerged rock off to the left. She held out her hand and hauled me onto it. That gave me a moment to compose myself. I put the mask on and put the tube in my mouth. Then, following her instruction, I lowered my head into the water and tried to breathe. In went a gulp of Lake Malawi shistasomiasis-soaked water.

"I am drinking in parasites," I thought. "I might as well have put them on my eggs this morning along with the salt and pepper."

I tried again. I got to where I could manage short water-free breaths. Still standing on the rock, I lowered my head into the lake and watched the fish gather around me. They were ciclids, some bright blue, others yellow striped, still others a mottled blue. I felt as if I were seeing an aquarium from the wrong side of the glass. They were quite beautiful. But I couldn't give them my undivided attention. The rock I was standing on was slippery and the flippers made me feel like a clown. I couldn't see the bottom. If I slipped off the rock and found that I couldn't swim with the flippers and started inhaling lake water at a great rate, I figured I would be in real trouble. I decided I had had enough.

I wanted to back up onto the rock-rimmed island fast. I could dry off, alcohol down, and hope that the water I had swallowed was non-parasitic. The rocks that made up the shoreline were covered with a slimy growth. They were like greased pigs. To make matters worse, they angled into the water. Every time I tried to haul myself up I slid back. I floundered around like a beached whale. I started to panic. If I slipped back into the water, I might sink straight down to the bottom. I could swim, but I wasn't all that confident about being able to swim with all this gear on. For an instant I had a vision of what I looked like to everyone watching. It was too ugly to contemplate. I went back to the comfort of panic. The boatman came running. He grabbed both my hands and unceremoniously hauled me up over the rocks like a sack of wet potatoes.

I made for the towel. Nancy said that my back looked like I had lost a fight with a cat. Both elbows were bleeding. So were one knee and both feet. I dried off. Nancy helped me apply alcohol and then Neosporin. I was acutely aware as I was being fussed over that everyone, all women and some embarrassingly older than me, had managed to snorkel without incident. At one point, the boatman tossed a handful of instant coffee into the water. The ciclids made for it like cats to catnip. Everyone rushed over to the edge to watch and I was left alone. Nancy came up to me. She asked me how I felt.

"Out of control," I said.

"You look it," she replied.

I think the reason Africa was so repellant to me was the picture I had of danger lurking everywhere. It never seemed to bother Nancy. When it was clear to me that Nancy was contemplating another trip to Africa, I would scour the newspapers for anti-African stories. The recurrence of Ebola was a bonanza for me. Outbreaks of this lethal hemorrhagic virus were certain to kill nine out of ten of its victims. The disease was shrouded in mystery. It attacked tourists who visited caves suggesting a connection with bats. It killed the owner of a nightclub, a different kind of cave. He had gone nowhere near a bat.

"We'll stay out of caves and nightclubs," she would say blithely.

"That's not the point. The point is you don't know where it comes from. Once it hits you, you're dead."

"If I thought like you," Nancy said. "I would never go anywhere."

I nodded vigorously.

If I wasn't born fearful, Pinker-style, then I acquired fearfulness at a very early age. Being a Jew born in 1935, I count myself incredibly lucky to have popped out of the birth canal in the United States and not some shtetl in Eastern Europe. Now it is only with the greatest reluctance that I leave home. Perhaps I am channeling the race memory of my ancestors. Why should I want to leave the place they sacrificed so much to get to?

Maybe. But I think that my travel paranoia is due in large part to a childhood spent in constant battle with other kids in an unfriendly neighborhood, a lower middle class, predominantly Catholic, neighborhood into which, because of the stock market crash and bankruptcy, my family was forced to move when I was five years old. Those childhood years accustomed me to the notion that it really was a jungle out there.

I don't really know the family history that well. My primary source was my mother. Her view of the family was skewed by an intense belief that my father's relatives were out to get her. Could I have made her agenda my own, substituting "everybody" for "my father's relatives"?

My mother told me that in the salad days of their marriage, my father had been the manager of a fancy hotel in Philadelphia, the St. James. They had a penthouse suite and an apartment outside the city for the weekends.

My father rarely spoke about his days as a manager. In fact, I remember just two things. The first was that the playwright Clifford Odets—he was born in Philadelphia—used to stay at my father's hotel. The second sounded like something out of an Odets play. One day a government agent came to the hotel to enlist my father's help in nailing the pharmacist next door. It was during Prohibition. If the pharmacist knew you, what came through the tap marked Soda was booze. My father told the agent he would be glad to help. When the agent left, my father went straight to the pharmacist and told him about the visit. From then on only soda water flowed through the fountain tap. My father had helped, though not in the fashion the agent expected.

A shrink once told me that I might never be able to appreciate how much I owed my father. He was, as is not untypical in many Jewish families, a mild-mannered, quiet, even-tempered, soft-spoken man married to a termagant. That is unfair to my mother. She was not a termagant. She just seemed like one. She was really a woman of great intelligence with virtually no internal resources, who had suffered a personal tragedy she never recovered from—the loss of a child, a year-old daughter who died 18 months before I was born due to a congenital heart defect. Her doctor advised her to have a hysterectomy. He wanted her out of the childbirth business. My mother would have none of it. She tried one last time. When I was born, the first thing she asked the doctor was, "How is his heart?" When the doctor said it was fine, she said, "O.K. you can take out my womb."

From then on Mom measured me against the golden yard-stick of her dead daughter. I always came up short. Once, in answer to his question about how the three of us interacted, I told my shrink that often when my mother started in on me, criticizing some shortcoming or other—perhaps I had failed to tuck in my shirt, or get a haircut, or choose the right friends—my father would interrupt by asking her a question.

"Like what?" my shrink asked.

"Like 'Who was Errol Flynn's first wife?'"

"Did she know the answer?" my shrink asked. He was curious. Not psychoanalytic.

"Invariably," I said. "My mother had an encyclopedic knowledge of Hollywood stars and their personal lives. He could always distract her with a question like that."

"Your father was a good man," my shrink answered. "By the way who was Flynn's first wife?"

"Lili Damita," I answered, or was I channeling mom?

Sabina Keyser and the author at 11 years of age sitting on the bumper of the family coupe circa 1946

The author, age 8, reflecting the innocence that comes with ignorance of a world in which travel and other evils exist.

My parents spent all their savings in a futile attempt to keep their daughter—her name was Suzanne—alive. As soon as the money ran out, fate delivered the second installment of its double whammy. My father was fired from his fancy job. My mother said he was fired because a Jewish real estate mogul had bought the hotel and, after converting to Catholicism for business reasons, fired my father because he was a Jew. Who knows? My mother was a bitter woman. Bitter people make bitter historians.

I was born a year after my father lost his job. He went to Washington, DC, to find work. My mother and I followed a couple of years later. My earliest memories are of life in Washington, DC, where I grew up, not in Philly where I was born.

When my mother and I first came to Washington to join my father, I was three and a half years old. We lived in a rooming house at 6th and Pennsylvania Avenue, SE. Our room was second floor front. The bathroom door—there was one bathroom for all the tenants—had a hook-and-eye lock that was well out of reach above my head. My mother always warned me never to lock the door when I went in. One day I closed the bathroom door behind me. Somehow the hook fell into the eye of its own accord. I was terrified. It wasn't just that I was locked in, but that I was locked in in spite of myself. I had followed my mother's instructions scrupulously. It made absolutely no difference. It was as if the hook had its own agenda. I was so much background noise. I started pounding on the door. I heard my mother on the other side. She told me to stand back. In the next instant the force of her shoulder against the door tore the hook and eye out of its socket. I was free.

Or was I? That incident is the earliest memory I have, the absolute first memory of my life on this planet. It ingrained in me my own version of *Murphy's Law*. Call it *Keyser's Corollary*. It says, "It doesn't matter whether the glass is half full or half empty because it's cracked."

Sometime after the bathroom incident and perhaps because of it, we rented a house next door to the Christ Episcopal Church at 6th and G Streets, SE. The church owned it. My father got a job as an accountant in an Oldsmobile dealership. (Now that GM has discontinued the line, I can hear the car door slamming on a part of my history.) The year was 1941. There was a war on. My mother went from being the mistress of two apartments to running a boarding house for shipyard workers at the Naval Ship Yard in southeast Washington.

I was too young to know how well she made the transition, but make it she did. Among my earliest memories are those of my mother throwing suitcases down the front stairs. They belonged to shipyard workers who had broken her only rule. Don't come in drunk.

Being the only Jewish kid on a decidedly Christian block, the responsibility for Christ's death fell squarely on my shoulders. My classmates called me Christ-killer. I owe them one. They provided me with the motivation to get the hell away from there. By dint of hard work, I was able to skip myself out of the neighborhood. I skipped two and a half grades. I would have skipped a third. The authorities found out that I was only 10 years old. They decided I was too young for junior high school.

Two brothers lived in my neighborhood. They were twins, skinny twins. They were several grades ahead of me. One day while I was walking to school, they waylaid me. They must have planned it for days. They jumped out from behind a hedge. One of them pinned my arms behind my back while the second lit a match and held it to my nose.

"We want to see if a Jew's nose burns," he said.

I yelled to a passerby for help. He kept going. The hook and eye in the bathroom taught me that the world was a dangerous place. The twins confirmed it, one of many such confirmations along the way growing up in a hostile neighborhood.

My mother was someone who loomed as large in my life as Large Marge did in Pee Wee Herman's Great Adventure. I shared my fifth grade class with a hulk of a classmate. He was a beefy boy twice as large as the rest of us. He liked to catch flies and pull off their wings. He knew whom he could torment with impunity. In the fifth grade it was flies and me. He sat directly behind me. Throughout the day he would uncap his fountain pen and jab me in the shoulder blade.

One afternoon after an especially severe barrage, I told my mother about him. I shouldn't have. It was against the neighborhood code of honor. Kids who told on other kids, especially to their mothers, were sissies. That is what I was. I was also tired of being a pincushion. I reasoned that if I confronted George—I still remember his name after 60 years— there would be a fight. It would take place during recess in the back of the school. Everyone would be watching. George would punch me in the face. My eyes would be blackened. My lips would be swollen. My nose would bleed. I would be thoroughly humiliated.

In my neighborhood there was no honor in fighting: only in winning. George's size and my timidity added up to a surefire loss for me. On top of which the next day George would uncork his fountain pen and I would be back to square one. I didn't see that I had that many options. So I told my mother.

The following day—it was during study period when everyone was supposed to be quiet—there was a noise at the classroom door. Someone was rattling the door handle. We all looked up. George had just landed a stinging blow to the back of my neck. When my mother walked in, my head was a hurricane of emotions, a lethal mix of elation that at last the cavalry had arrived and public humiliation that my mother had to settle my scores for me.

Without a glance at the teacher she walked over to the desk behind me. She didn't even stop to look at me.

"Are you George?" she asked.

I assumed he nodded. I was too ashamed to turn around.

"George, if you ever touch my son again, I'll beat the shit out of you. Is that clear?"

She didn't look at me once. She just walked out, leaving the class, the teacher, and me in stunned silence.

I never forgave my mother or myself for that humiliating day. On the other hand George never touched me again. Back then I thought it was a terrible deal. Today I thank my lucky stars I had the good sense to tell my mother. The downside was that as long as she was alive, I felt as if I were carrying a protective amulet around with me, like the evil eye or a bag of asafetida around my neck. Once she died, I was out there on my own. Now nothing stood between me and the Georges of the world.

I lay my paranoia at the feet of my history of growing up in a tough neighborhood, my separation from my father for the first three and a half years of my life, and a shorter than average D4DR dopamine receptor gene, the one that separates the risk takers from the risk avoiders. After 60 years of worrying about malevolent matchbook-laden twins hiding in the shadows, fate married me to a woman with a love of the bush and the soul of a machete.

Nancy takes risks that don't at all seem to her to be risks. The first time this came home to me was in Sienna. We had climbed to the top of the Campanile in the town square, the Piazza del Campo. The bell tower is 285 feet high. At the very top are narrow unprotected openings. The slits are wide enough to haul yourself up into them. When Nancy and I reached this part of the Campanile, I was already suffering from the height. I refused to look out without first getting a firm grip on something—a pipe, a grill, Nancy. Nancy would have none of it. She shook herself loose, hauled herself up into the opening in the wall, and leaning her back against the side, she pushed her feet against the opposite side to wedge herself in. Then she leaned out over the edge and began to photograph the piazza 285 feet below. Just thinking about it now knots my stomach.

"Come down before you fall," I pleaded.

"Can't you see I'm photographing?" she barked.

It was too hard to stand there and watch. If she wouldn't come down, then I would. I climbed down the steps to the platform below and hoped that she would reappear.

Every time Nancy picks a new destination, she is picking a new set of tormentors for my imagination to reckon with. I travel with one eye on the road ahead and one looking over my shoulder. If that sounds uncomfortable, then you understand.

CHAPTER 7

Don't Step over This Line

Female gorilla in Bwindi Impenetrable Forest, Buhoma,
Uganda, flirting with the author.

On a 2004 trip to Africa, there were eight of us—six women, me and another male. The other male was already off to a bad start in my book when he announced that he was going to leave the safari early. I somehow felt he was abandoning me, let alone his wife. Even while he was there, he was never really there. One afternoon all of us were sitting in a dining tent somewhere in the Serengeti National Park. It was late afternoon. We had come back from a day of watching the wildebeest migration, that incredible river of gnus that ebbs and flows between Tanzania and Kenya in search of food and water. Over 1.5 million of the animals flood the countryside. In the first quarter of each year, they add to their numbers by cloning themselves anywhere from 300,000 to 400,000 times. They literally rain calves on the savannah.

On this particular afternoon the animals had stopped for the evening. You could tell because the flies that accompany them everywhere had begun to collect around us, a sure sign that wildebeest were in the neighborhood. We all had a drink in our hands. The women were sharing stories. Someone described how she had seen a calf's hind legs protruding from its mother's backside. Someone else saw a wildebeest sound asleep in the middle of the road. In the midst of all this rehashing, my male companion got up, walked outside the tent, pulled out a satellite telephone the size of a shoebox, and called London. He was setting up a meeting for the next day. Talk about not being in the moment. The women, of course, weren't scandalized by his behavior. I believe they thought of him the way a mother might think of a child fidgeting inside a museum.

He was like most of the guys I've rubbed shoulders with on safaris. Whatever they want, it certainly isn't what women want. At a camp in the foothills of Kilimanjaro, I overheard a woman and five men—actually four men and a teenage boy—talking about their week in Tanzania. (They were leaving the next day.) The men had climbed to the top of Kilimanjaro and were rolling the experience around on their gin-scented tongues.

"Been there, done that," said one.

"Straight to the top in three-and-a-half days," said another.

I introduced myself and asked the men to tell me what it was like climbing to the top of Kilimanjaro. They talked about the achievement, not the experience. I came away from that conversation knowing only that they made it to the summit and that it took them seven days up and back. I had no idea how the sunrise looked from the mountain, how the mornings smelled, how it felt to climb 20,000 feet in three days, and neither, I suspect, did they. Clearly, they were goal-oriented people, just like me. It gave me pause. Maybe, like them, I needed to stop and smell the elephant droppings.

Sometimes I do: on the shores of Lake Ndutu I watched one early morning, sleep still tugging hard at me, as a fleet of open safari vehicles, mostly Land Cruisers, convened at the lakeshore where the usual Noah's ark of animals had begun to assemble: endless zebras, bewildered beests, giraffe, elephant, the occasional lion, to say nothing of augur buzzards, martial and bateleur eagles, and black-winged shrikes. The vehicles were filled with women gazing intently at this animal or that, cameras at the ready. They were literally vibrating with energy. Their faces were flushed. They were animated, excited, whispering to one another with such intensity it sounded as if a swarm of bees had invaded the Land Cruiser. I had never seen them so vibrant, certainly not back home. That was especially true of Nancy. She was so engaged with life at that moment that I was jealous of the animals. Come to think of it, I still am.

Now very much awake, I turned to our guide, Peter Jones.

"What in hell is going on? I don't get it. They are having the time of their lives."

"It's the spell of Africa," he said.

"And what is that?" I asked.

"Being back where everything began. If this is the environment in which our most basic instincts were formed, then coming back here is getting back in touch with who we are." And then, after a moment's thought, he added, "I think women actually come here to hunt, only they do it with cameras."

Peter is an extremely competent and highly respected safari guide. He first came to Tanzania in 1976 to work with Mary and Richard Leakey for a summer. He ended up staying. He was with the team that uncovered the Laetoli footprints,

105

working at the site where Mary Leakey found *Australopithecus afarensis*. She had been walking her pet Dalmatian when she had the good fortune to see a tooth sticking out of a dusty hillside.

The Laetoli footprints—a large set, obviously a male and a smaller set, a female—are preserved in a 25-meter strip of volcanic ash hardened by a light rain and then preserved by a second ash fall from a nearby eruption of the volcano called Sadiman. There is evidence of a third creature, another male, following close behind. The female's feet are splayed as if she were carrying a load. Perhaps she was pregnant. Perhaps she was carrying an infant on her hip. Whatever she was doing, she was doing it 3.6 million years ago. The leading male and female must have had their arms around one another. Their footprints are that close together. These are the earliest examples of bipedal gaited creatures in paleontological history. Peter was there when they were discovered.

He described to me what happened. It was toward the end of the day. A couple of the excavators were tossing elephant dung at one another. I imagine that's what one does after a frustrating day of scratching around in the earth and finding nothing. One of the excavators, Andrew Hill, ducked and in the ducking saw the outlines of the footprints right there on the surface. They were staring him in the foot.

The footprints were found in the Olduvai Gorge, a gorge in the heart of the Great African Rift. The rift is actually a huge trench extending from one end of the continent to the other, a trench that was formed millions of years ago and is still sinking. The eastern escarpment—the wall formed by

Peter Jones, safari guide, and young Maasai
goatherd exchanging greetings outside a Maasai village (boma) in the Engaruka Plain, near
Arusha, Tanzania.

the sinking rift—is 15 million years old. The western escarpment is comparatively recent, maybe 3 million years old.

The difference in the birthdays of these two walls has
played a critical role in the development of the human race.
Prior to the Rift Valley coming into being, the entire area
of Uganda, Kenya, and Tanzania was a heavily forested
land where tree-dwelling animals like the chimpanzee, the
gorilla, and the monkey evolved. With the rise of the western

escarpment, a rain shadow cast its pall over the forested area, raising the temperature and turning the forest east of the western escarpment into savannah. The chimps, the apes, the monkeys all followed the receding forest west. But some of their ancestors mutated into savannah dwellers; for example, the 3.6-million-year olds whose footprints were discovered at Laetoli, those hominids who—just like us—don't have a huge gap between the big toe and the index toe. In other words we owe our lives to the Great African Rift Valley. I can't think of a better example of the symbiosis that exists between life on earth and the Earth itself.

In out-of-the-way places like the Bwindi Impenetrable Forest, my intuitions about what is safe and what isn't are as useful as galoshes on a camel. In order to see the gorillas, you have to gather in a central place, a kind of Bwindi Impenetrable Forest headquarters. That's where you are given walking sticks, divided up into groups, hire porters, are introduced to your guides, and begin the long, hard slog up into the forest. Before setting out on our 2007 quest for gorillas, our guide told us that the day before a solitary male had challenged the silverback we would be tracking. The solitary lost. The silverback led his band deeper into the forest. We had to walk 13 miles to find them—seven impenetrable miles in and six out.

The locals call the hills where the gorillas live the Switzerland of Uganda. Mountains they are not. High they are. When we started out, two trackers came with us. These were the guys skilled at finding gorillas. Along with them came two soldiers carrying automatic rifles. One took up a position at the front, the second at the rear. They never spoke to us and stayed at the edges of the activity. I wondered why soldiers with guns. I didn't ask. Nancy didn't have to.

We were encouraged to hire a porter to carry our gear and to push and pull us up over the rough spots. I thought about declining. I didn't like the idea of someone carrying my gear for me. It seemed so unegalitarian. Thank goodness I went ahead with it. For one thing the porters badly needed the money. For another I badly needed the porters.

I didn't choose Perry. She chose me. She was 19 years old. She had just finished high school and was applying to college. This was how she was earning tuition money. She was a short, stocky, powerful looking woman. We were all standing around in a circle waiting for the porters to come over. Suddenly, she appeared in front of me like a pop-up box on the Internet. There was no way I was going to say no to her and pick a male. First, I didn't want to offend her. Second, I was flattered that she chose me. Third, she seemed by far the most powerful porter in the lot. So Perry and I bonded. I used what little Lugandan I knew to break the ice.

"Olyotya gendi (How are you, ma'm?)", I said. "Mkono tokimenya (Don't break my arm.)."

"Very pleased to meet you," she responded in perfect English.

We climbed to the crest of the first hill. The trail switched back and forth as if the God of Zorro had laid it out with his wonderful whip. Where the trail changed direction, there was often a three-foot-high step. Perry got behind me and with her hand in the small of my back pushed me up to the next level as if I were a rag doll. It was close to 12 noon when we got to the top of the hill. The ascent had taken three hours. We stopped for a water break. It was extremely hot. I was exhausted from the climb and the heat. I found a tree to lean against. I didn't dare sit down. It would have been hard to get back up.

After a few minutes we started a descent into the valley beyond the crest. Someone hailed Joseph, the lead tracker, on the walkie-talkie. Apparently, the gorillas had reversed direction. They were moving back toward the village. We climbed back up to the crest. By this time it was already one o'clock. If we didn't find the gorillas in the next hour, we would have to slink out of the forest without a sighting. You can't risk being caught in the Impenetrable Forest after dark. We followed a ridge for several minutes. Joseph stopped us.

"The gorillas are only 300 feet away," he said. "We are going to go off-track."

The idea was to cut through a thicket to save time. The gorillas were on the other side, barely a football field away. By now we had been trekking for four and a half hours. I was beginning to understand what running on empty meant. Every step was painful. Perry was close behind. Every so often she would thrust a water bottle at me and tell me to drink. I didn't argue.

The trackers started hacking a passage through a thicket of stinging nettles, thorn bushes, and climbing vines. This was the part of the climb where the tough were supposed to get going because the going had certainly gotten tough. The forest had a mind of its own. Every step was impeded by a thorn, sometimes into my socks, sometimes into my sleeve, and at least once each into my forehead and leg. The level of difficulty of the climb had ratcheted up. The needle was teetering precariously between very difficult and an ordeal. The heat wasn't making it any easier, on top of which I was, as instructed, wearing thick leather gloves against the nettle stings.

Finally, we came out into a clearing.

"They are here," Joseph whispered.

I looked around. All I saw were thickets, thorn bushes and flying insects as fat and green as lima beans. I glimpsed a dark shadow deep inside a bower. It didn't look like a thorn bush. But it didn't look like a gorilla either. I looked up quizzically. A female gorilla was standing seven feet away. She stood on all fours blinking at me as if I were an optometrist's eye chart. We stared at one another for a full minute. It was an extraordinary minute, seeing a creature separated from me by ten million years of evolution, but a relative nonetheless.

An African guide once told me that when you look into the eyes of a lion you see cold gold. That is perfectly true. No one or no thing appears to be inside looking out. But when you look into the eyes of a gorilla, it is a completely different story. Someone's home.

A second female suddenly appeared on my left, rolling out of the underbrush like a can of coke out of a soft drink machine. She came to a halt on her back. She raised her arms fetchingly over her head and gave me a come-hither look that was unnerving. I have absolutely no doubt she was flirting with me. I felt flattered. A larger female rolled into view. She was clutching a tiny male to her bosom. Only his bottom half was visible. The baby was seven weeks old. The mother had presented herself for grooming and that is what the flirtatious gorilla proceeded to do, leaving me on the forest floor like so much vegetable detritus.

I watched her work her way through the mother's hair. The small motor control of her fingers—that is exactly what they were, fingers—was just like my own. She lifted the hair with one finger, raised it again, inspected the patch of skin underneath and, satisfied, moved on. If she found something, she delicately picked it out between two fingers and ate it. Then she continued up or, in this case, down the torso. Soon she was inspecting the female's genitalia with the same equanimity that she exhibited on her belly. I was embarrassed for her. I looked away. Then I looked back. The female had made no fastidious distinction among the body parts of her companion. I did. Shame on me. But that is the point of original sin, isn't it? An inability to credit innocence.

Throughout all this I had only the merest glimpse of the silverback. He had kept his distance, resting deep inside the dark thicket like a Pooh-bah. When I peered in with my binoculars, I could see his flat, massive face. His eyes were open. He was staring at his fingers. A low-pitched rumble bubbled up from deep within his chest signaling to the band that all was well. The guides mimicked that sound from time to time to send the same message. From my vantage point I had no sense of the silverback's size. I knew he had to be large, larger than the largest female, but nothing prepared me for the full impact of his bulk. He weighed at least 500 pounds. He was six feet long in the torso. Add another two feet when he stands up on his hind legs, which are, of course, shorter than his arms. Were he, for whatever reason, to raise his arms above his head, I would give him 12 feet from stem to stern.

I only saw him for a few seconds, half a minute at the most. He was up and out of there as if he were late for an appointment. But I would have to give those 30 seconds the blue ribbon for being the most respectful 30 seconds I have spent in Africa.

My reaction at seeing a gorilla without a cage mediating between us was complicated; a mixture of two parts incredulity and three parts awe. Here was a creature whose genome and mine overlapped 98.7 percent of the time. Look at the similarity, its hands so like mine, its face so like mine. The small motor control the female juveniles displayed when they groomed one another suggests their motor cortex and mine are alike. We have made eye contact. Yet what a difference 1.3 percent has made. It has given us language, which has given us history, which has meant that the dead of our species can talk to the living.

When I am on safari, I stand well behind the photographers. I don't need to position myself at just the right angle for this shot or that aspect. Generally, it keeps me out of trouble. Not this time. Backing away from the photographic action, I invaded the comfort zone of another female. She was sitting on the thick grass mat of the forest plucking at the tender parts of a nettle bush. Perhaps she thought I had my eye on her nettle. She showed me the ugly side of her personality. She jumped to her feet, bared her teeth, and snarled. To make sure the point wasn't lost, she karate-chopped a branch in front of her, breaking it in two as if to say, "Come any closer and this is what will happen to you."

I jumped back.

"Don't worry," said a nearby tracker. "She's just warning you."

Uncharacteristically, I wasn't worried. I had this remarkable sensation of having communicated with a wild animal. She had indicated displeasure. I reacted the way she wanted. She acknowledged my reaction by sinking back down into the heap of her body and re-addressing the nettle bush. A transaction, if not exactly a conversation, had transpired between us. I felt as if we had gotten to know one another better. Nothing like this had ever happened before between me and an animal—the single exception being my dog, Tuppence, who lived with me for five years some 40 years ago before a car put an end to her.

Tuppence was a product of my first marriage, bought as a companion for the children and my first wife. Very quickly Tuppence attached herself to me. Though she was friendly with my wife and my daughters, it was clear that I was the apple of her eye. For months I tried unsuccessfully to teach her tricks. Then one day it was as if a light bulb had gone off over her head.

Oh! That's what you want me to do.

Soon I had Tuppence counting to ten, rolling over and playing dead, shaking hands. I would spread my legs like a colossus and slap my thigh. She would walk between them. That was called "under the bridge." There was no end to the tricks I could teach her and no end to the times I would show her off at dinner parties. Then, one day it occurred to me that making Tuppence do all these party tricks was demeaning. Like a drug addict gone cold turkey, I stopped. We drew even closer. She was there when I was working, there when I went to sleep, there when I woke up. On Christmas Eve she was across the street when I came out of the house to bring in some packages. She ran across to greet me. A car ran over her. The driver didn't stop. Tuppence ran around in circles in front of me, literally screaming like a human being. Then she died. I called the town immediately. A truck came by within 20 minutes and carted her away.

It's odd that I would have thought of Tuppence when that juvenile female was showing me her teeth. But then again maybe it wasn't.

We were only allowed an hour with the gorillas. Then it was time to go back, though not the way we came. We would have been caught in the Impenetrable Forest after dark. Instead, we climbed to the top of the hill whose valley we were in. Then, it was a straight descent at a 20° angle to the banana plantation below and its attendant village. The descent was extremely hard. On private property the owner had refused to allow the trail to be switch-backed. He was obliged to provide an escape route for parties like ours but reluctant to give any more of his land to it than he had to. This was the part of the climb where Perry, my porter, was indispensable. More than once she stopped me from tumbling head over heels. Whenever she sensed me losing my balance, she planted her foot on the path and became a wall that I could lean against.

Even with Perry's help, the 13-mile trek in and out of the Impenetrable Forest was close to the edge of my ability. I had reached that stage in life—I was 71 years old—when age mattered. The years no longer spread out in front of me like a Kansas highway: straight, unbending, inexhaustible. I could glimpse the end of the road. It was not a thought I especially liked.

After we got back to camp, I felt something I had never felt before as a traveler. Certainly I was pleased with myself. I had paid a big physical price to see the gorillas. I would never have thought a safari could offer me a sense of accomplishment. This one did. Still there was something more. Anxiety at being in an unfamiliar and dangerous place was trumped by an emotional impact that I couldn't have experienced anyplace else. I had had an encounter with a distant relative, a female gorilla. I felt some kind of connection if only that we were related, that we both shared a common ancestor, the creature from which the gorilla on the one hand and the chimpanzee and *Homo sapiens* on the other had descended 13 millions years ago. To have seen her and her companions where she lived and not where I lived made all the difference. I was an enthralled guest, she an enigmatic hostess.

As I battled my way out of the forest it occurred to me that the first person in the real sense of "person" had to have sprung from a parent who looked to her the way the chimp or the gorilla looked to us. The creature had the potential to think in words. Her parents literally could never know what she was thinking about. In other words *Homo sapiens* was born alienated. That strikes me as the real meaning behind the myth of Adam and Eve in the Garden of Eden. At any rate that is what I took with me when I managed to walk out of the Bwindi Impenetrable Forest. That and, at long last, an inkling of why it is that I follow Nancy into impenetrable places despite everything.

CHAPTER 8

It's Only As Good As Your Guide

Lily, China tour guide.

Whenever travelers of my generation get together, they compare notes about their trips. The conversation inevitably begins with an assessment of how lucky they were when it came to tour leaders. It is an axiom of travel that one's trip is only as good as one's guide.

I have definitely found this to be true. In Burma, a junta ruled state if ever there were one, our guide was as honest as he was excellent. In fact, he was so open about the Burmese government's oppressive corruption that when I wrote about him in my journal, I didn't use his real name. I called him Q after James Bond's armorer. He wasn't going to end up in some military jail on my account.

Then there was Lemalale, also known as "Kidogo," 'little one' in Swahili. He was our guide when we visited the Maasai Steppes in Tanzania. Lemalale is a Dorobo, a tribe that is slowly disappearing because the number of eligible brides is shrinking. Dorobo women were marrying Maasai men. Soon, like a puddle after rain, the Dorobos will disappear. Twenty years ago some 600 were alive. Today that number has almost certainly gone down.

Peter Jones, our African guide in Kenya, who was there when the Laetoli footprints were discovered, hired Lemalale to do an impossible job. Jones, an honorary Dorobo, was keeping business in the family. He had bought land between

Mount Meru and Kilimanjaro to build his own African resort, Ndarakwai. The land was infested with deadly black mambas. Peter hired Lemalale to get rid of them. This he did, wearing rubber flip-flops made out of old tire tread and with a very sharp knife. Where St. Patrick and the Irish snakes were the stuff of myths, Lemalale was the real thing. The Dorobos are known to be especially good with knives. The Maasai hire them to perform circumcisions.

Now that I think about them, the names of my past guides rain down in my mind like confetti in a ticker tape parade: Sonia of Egypt, Jeff and Brian of Botswana, Bantok of Bali, Chencho of Bhutan, Claudio of Easter Island, Mohammed of Morocco, Robin of Zambia, David of Malawi, Zuberi of Kenya. They were all extraordinary people. Some had college degrees and were working as guides because it was the only work available. Some combined guide work with academic research wearing two hats. Some had pulled themselves up by the bootstraps, became expert birders, historians, equestrians, trackers and turned themselves into guides because that was were the money was.

And then there was Chinese Lily (not her real name). She was a bright, warm-hearted, sprite of a guide. She spoke fluent English, passable Dutch—her husband was Dutch—and fluent French—she spent several years in Paris. She was in her mid-thirties when I met her. The wonder is that China could have produced such a ray of Chinese sunshine given her family history.

I imagine all these great guides have a backstory. Here is Lily's. When her father was seven years old, his father died of

a cerebral hemorrhage. Left to his own devices the son somehow became a servant in the house of a Kuomintang officer.
He was eight years old. He worked there for a year. At nine
he left to go into business selling peanuts on street corners.
At 16 he joined the army. By then the early stirrings of Mao's
Cultural Revolution had begun. The year was 1961. Mao's
purification police found out about his year as a Kuomintang
officer's eight year old servant. Nothing short of full scale
cleansing would do. He was booted out of the army.

He found work in a local college where he taught Marx-
ist philosophy. In 1967, one year after the official launching
of the Cultural Revolution, he was deemed insufficiently
cleansed and was sent to the countryside to learn from the
peasants. As ill luck would have it, his wife was hospitalized
when he went off to the countryside. That left Lily's nine-
year-old sister and her five-year-old brother at home to fend
for themselves.

One day her brother wandered away from the house. He
seemed to have disappeared into thin air. Her father was
permitted to come back from the countryside to help in the
search. The next morning the boy was found floating face
down in a water-filled tunnel that had been built during
the 1950s to protect the Chinese from an American atomic
bomb attack. The shock of losing her son was too much for
the mother. She died a few months later of a heart attack. All
of this happened because a year of service in the home of a
Kuomintang officer at the age of eight was deemed morally
debilitating. The duty of a father to look after his children
was trumped by the rectitude of the Red Guard.

Lily's father married his dead wife's sister. Lily was born in 1973, three years before the end of the Cultural Revolution. Lily experienced none of its atrocities. Her father told her she was born in a honeycomb. Her sister, now a successful restaurateur, remains deeply cynical about the government, its past and its future. Her father, still a teacher of Communist philosophy and a member of the Communist party, remains loyal to both. There may have been mistakes, he thinks, but in the end it was good for the people. As for Lily, she doesn't care about politics. All she wants is to be left alone to show people like Nancy and me the China she grew up in.

Not all my experiences with guides have been upbeat. One of the most unnerving occurred after we had flown from Nairobi, Kenya to the Meru National Park 270 miles away. We were all scheduled to drive overland, but one of our group suffered from severe motion sickness whenever she had to drive long distances. Nancy and I had agreed to fly to the Meru along with our susceptible companion and her friends. Our plane, a Beechcraft Baron, had two 270 horsepower engines capable of speeds upwards of 180 knots. We would cover the distance in a mere 45 minutes. As the Swahili expression has it: *hakuna matata* 'no problem.'

Charles was a typical bush pilot. He was good-looking—what romance novels would call dashing—extremely friendly and thin as a rail. About ten minutes into the flight he motioned out the starboard window. In the distance, clouds streaming from its peak like water from a breaching whale, was the hump of Mt. Kenya. Seventeen thousand feet high, it is the highest volcano in Kenya. From our airborne vantage point, its shape was peculiar, a normal peak, smooth and rounded off at the top and then, in the middle of that rounded shoulder, jutting up like a gigantic thumb, was a huge rock formation, so steep and sheer that it can't be climbed. It looked as if the mountain were trying to hitch a ride.

When our landing site came into view, I saw that it was nothing but a long strip of aging concrete with grass growing up between the cracks and what looked like piles of brush strewn about its surface. Before we landed, Charles buzzed the strip. What I had taken to be brush turned out to be sleeping baboons and gazelles attracted by the warmth of the concrete. They scattered like leaves before a leaf blower.

Charles eased the plane into a perfect three-point touchdown. When we came to a stop, he apologized for the bumpy landing. My last two bush pilots did exactly the same thing. I think this must be what bush pilots always say at the end of a beautifully executed maneuver. It is like Sam Irvin during Nixon's impeachment hearings telling reporters he was just a country lawyer.

It was 10 AM. No one was at the airstrip. Charles didn't want to leave us unattended in the middle of the Meru. So he waited until the characteristic brown Land Cruiser from African Expeditions drove up a half hour later. We said our goodbyes. He jumped into his Beechcraft Baron and was off.

As he disappeared into the clouds, I felt my usual anxiety skittering around inside me like a hamster inside a wheel. He had left us in a desolate spot with a desolate history. This was where Joy Adamson and her husband lived and worked until they separated in 1971. This is where she raised and wrote about Elsa, the lioness. Her book, *Born Free,* focused world attention on African wildlife preservation. Then, in 1980, a disgruntled worker killed her. Nine years after that, poachers murdered her ex-husband.

None of this was lost on me as we moved toward a decaying building at the end of the field, the Meru Miluka Lodge. Our guide, Peter, who had come to meet us, thought we might like to inspect the lodge before we drove to camp. It was still very early. Those of us who were driving wouldn't catch up for hours.

We walked to the lodge at the end of the airstrip. The decrepit building squatted in the sunlight. It seemed to be disintegrating before our eyes. The thatched roof had a hole in it. The lounge, once quite fashionable, even hip, was a trash heap of chairs, tables and broken glass. Through the panoramic window at the far end, I saw a herd of a hundred water buffalo grazing placidly in a field just beyond.

In better days this may have been a watering hole for those African tourists who shelled out $50,000 to put a bullet into one of the ancestors of the animals that lay about the airstrip this morning. The bar still had a display of wine bottles hanging from an artificial vine. They had never been uncorked. The liquid inside had faded to a diluted cranberry. The place was like a ghost town in an old cowboy movie where the shutters clattered in the same wind that pushed tumbleweed down Main Street. Three Maasai tribesmen guarded the lodge. Why, I wondered.

We piled into the Land Cruiser and drove off toward camp. At least we thought that is what we were doing. After a while it seemed that Peter was dawdling. Nothing in his driving was authoritative. We told him, after he made a few stops for us to see the odd zebra, giraffe or waterbuck, that we were anxious to get to the camp because one of us suffered from motion sickness. She was already beginning to feel queasy. We explained that she needed to stop moving and lie down as soon as possible.

Oddly, Peter didn't seem to get the picture. Instead of heading directly to the camp he would turn down a road, stop, turn the vehicle around and go back the way we came. I told him a second time that we really needed to get back, that our companion was feeling ill. He nodded and turned the vehicle around yet again. Something strange was going on.

One of us thought that maybe he was delaying because the tents weren't ready. We discussed that for a bit. We came to the conclusion that, even if it were true, our motion sick companion didn't need a tent. A simple cot would do. By this time she was lying flat in the back seat moaning softly. Once again we urged Peter to make tracks for the camp. Peter looked very uncomfortable. Nancy suggested we ask him to make a pit stop and that I use the opportunity to take him aside and find out what was going on.

I managed to get Peter to walk with me so that we were out of earshot of the Land Cruiser. I broached the subject as tactfully as I knew how.

"You're lost! Right, Peter?"

He looked down wriggling his foot as if it were caught in a cattle guard.

"Hakuna matata," I said. "We'll find find our way back."

We returned to the Land Cruiser. I broke the news. Our queasy companion groaned.

"I'm sure we can find our own way," I said as cheerfully as I knew how to no one in particular.

Nancy found an ersatz map of the area in her knapsack. She handed it to me—like I was some kind of pathfinder. It was a Xerox copy of a schematic map from the *Lonely Planet*, Kenya edition. I read the small print under the map. The Meru National Park is so rarely visited, it said, that one could go for days without seeing another vehicle. I decided not to share that with my companions.

Peter pointed to where he thought the camp was. I said that wouldn't be much help until we knew how to orient the map. One of us remembered that he had a U.S. government-issue compass in his backpack. Compass in hand I walked up the road away from the metallic bulk of the Land Cruiser. I made an effort to look like I knew what I was doing. It was a pathetic display. Here I was in the middle of the Meru National Park in the middle of Kenya with a guide who was supposed to know which way was up and I was looking at a schematic map in a guide book that was put there by someone in page makeup who must have thought this would look nice at the top of the page and hadn't the slightest idea that some-day someone might need it to save his skin. My worst fears were coming true. How long until nightfall when the animals come out, I wondered.

The compass looked like an old-fashioned pocket watch. Its pointer was in the shape of an arrow with a pointed head and a v-shaped tail. I turned the map so that the top coincided with what the compass indicated was north. I tried to plot a route from where I thought we were to where Peter thought the camp was. Talk about the blind leading the blind.

I started to explain to everyone what we were about to do when the compass owner said, "I tried that compass out back home. The tail points north, not the head."

I handed him the compass and said, "Let's see if we can find someone."

By now it was two o'clock in the afternoon, some three hours after we had left the airstrip. Suddenly we came to a clearing with a number of abandoned buildings in it. An ancient face appeared in one of the windows of the nearest building. It disappeared as quickly as it had popped up, like the gatekeeper in the Wizard of Oz.

In the next instant a tiny old man, thin as a rail and dressed only in a shirt and pants, no shoes, appeared beside the hut. He told us his name was Bennett. Peter engaged him in extended conversation. There was a lot of pointing of fingers and swirling motions of the arms.

Now Peter was energized. He set out along a new track, this one a barely perceptible road just to the side of the clearing. About a half mile up the road, the track disappeared beneath a fast flowing stream. It was much too deep for the Land Cruiser. We turned back to where we had left the little old man.

Bennett said he was certain he knew where the camp was. I took a seat in the back so Bennett could more easily direct Peter. A half hour later it became abundantly clear that, like Peter, Bennett also didn't have a clue. He had just come along for the ride. That was why he put a faded striped suit jacket on over his shirt and pants before coming with us. He had dressed for an outing.

We decided that perhaps we should go back to the airstrip and ask the tribesmen guarding the lodge for directions. They were no more knowledgeable than Bennett. By now people's spirits were sagging with the exception of Bennett's. He was happy as a clam at high tide. Peter, on the other hand, was miserable. He began passing his hand over the top of his head as if he were shooing away flies.

At last we found a sign pointing the way to one of the park gates. Maybe someone there would know about the camp. A slim guard, dressed in ranger green with a thick web belt around a wasp waist, greeted us as we drove up. He and Peter launched into lengthy discussion. While they were at it, another guard, no more than a teenager, approached. He was dressed just like his companion only without the webbed belt.

I no longer trusted Peter to get any useful information from anyone. So in English I asked the young man if he knew where the camp was.

"Sure," he said.

"Will you take us there if we bring you back?"

"Sure," he said.

The young man fetched his AK 47 and squeezed in next to Bennett.

"Are we going somewhere where we'll be needing that?" I asked the young man.

He said that it was always good to have a gun in the Meru National Park. Fifteen minutes later we ran into the first vehicle we had seen in five hours, a Land Cruiser just like ours. Simon, a camp staffer, and his driver were in it. They were out, of course, looking for us. We were, after all, five hours late.

Bennett climbed into Simon's vehicle. The driver promised to take him back to the clearing where he lived alone, but not uneventfully. As Bennett passed in front of the windscreen of our vehicle, he raised both his arms above his head in a victory salute.

Our teenage guard transferred to a second vehicle and in a matter of minutes he, too, was gone. Ten minutes after that we were in camp where Peter Senior, the camp master, was waiting, his face a collage of concern and relief.

"We were so worried," he said. "You are so late."

I told him we had had a great afternoon, thanks to Peter. Everyone agreed. We did this to protect Peter. It was useless. I saw the chilling look the camp master had given him. The afternoon had cost Peter his job.

The saddest story of all is about Cliff Kisitu, a guide who took me through Uganda. Cliff would have made Dale Carnegie (*How to Win Friends and Influence People*) look like an amateur. He was almost six-feet tall with a head shaved clean as an 8-ball. He had a muscular body but with just the slightest hint of a paunch. He looked like an African Mr. Clean. He knew twenty Ugandan languages and dialects and was able to converse with everyone we ran into as we made our way across Uganda to the Bwindi Impenetrable Forest, whether it was the cow-herder who threw rocks at us because we were taking his photograph and therefore his soul or whether it was the moonshiner producing *warragi* from a portable still that he carried on his back as he staggered out of the woods and into the road we were driving on.

Once when I had been dozing in the front seat, Cliff suddenly stopped the Land Cruiser in front of a rural school. The children were in recess outside. As soon as he stopped, they hid. Cliff called to them in their own dialect. Their shyness melted away. What did he say to them? Free chocolate bars? Whatever it was, they came bounding out of the schoolyard and gathered next to the vehicle. Their teacher hurried after them, concern furrowing her brow. It was too late. Cliff and his special magic had wrested control.

"Can you sing us a song?" he asked in the local language, Luchiga.

Like a gas burner that bursts into flame at the touch of a match, the entire class burst into song led by Cliff clapping and chanting rhythmically as if he had been their very own choral director for years.

A young girl stepped out in front. She was dressed in a thin, threadbare smock that hung off her shoulders like a blouse on a hangar.

She started to sing, "I am the youngest star."

The entire group responded, "So what?"

She went on singing, all the while performing a little dance, poking the air with her index fingers, first one hand, then the other, while she traced a shuffling circle in the dust.

"I sing all over the mountain. I sing, sing, sing all over. I sing all over Uganda."

Before she had finished, another girl stepped forward. The

song went on. The students sang for the sheer joy of it, their faces suffused with pleasure, their white-toothed smiles shining like flashlights.

At first the teacher had her hand to her face in a gesture of consternation mixed with worry. Apparently, the poise, the grace, the easy camaraderie of her charges put all that to rest. When I looked at her a second time, her face was alive with pride. I really don't think she knew they could do that. That was the kind of guide Cliff was. They probably didn't know that themselves until he came along.

Cliff pressed some money into the teacher's hand.

"Buy them all a pencil," he said.

Then he jumped into the Land Cruiser and we drove away, leaving them to ask one another, "Who was that masked man?"

That was a typical Cliff Kisitu party trick. He had that ineffable ability to pull a memory out of thin air and leave it to thrive inside our heads.

Early on in our Ugandan trip—the date was February 23, 2007—we took a boat ride to Murchison Falls. The Falls are on the Victoria Nile, that part of the Nile River that flows for 300 miles northwest out of Lake Victoria. In the lower part of the river a series of rapids culminate in this impressively dangerous part of the Nile. Eleven thousand cubic feet of water per second tear through a narrow 23-foot gap and drop 141 feet into a 30-foot wide gorge. The result is a massive upsurge of water that the locals call the Devil's Cauldron. The surge is so threatening that tour boats prudently stop a quarter of a mile away.

Our boat was a narrow hulled riverboat, powered by a

60 horsepower Evinrude engine. We sat in molded plastic seats as if we were outdoors at a floating Taco Bell restaurant. A rigid awning was overhead. The sides were open. The name of the boat was the Shoebill, aptly named after the prehistoric-looking Shoebill stork. Our boatman nosed the craft up against a tiny island in the middle of the river. Ahead of us was the raging torrent of the Devil's Cauldron. Next to us was a large rock. Perched on it completely oblivious to the furor just ahead were two rock pratincols. They were sleek birds, tiny, with beaks like stilettoes. Their wings were black, their chests white, and they had narrow bands of black across their eyes so that they looked like a pair of Nike brand running shoes.

According to *The Field Guide to the Birds of East Africa,* pratincols are typically found on rocks by fast moving bodies of water. Given the rate at which the water was rushing past this rock, these birds must have thought they had died and gone to bird heaven. I couldn't possibly have known that five years later our guide, Cliff Kisitu, would do just that and in just this place.

Here is a paragraph from the *Ugandan Daily Monitor* dated April 12, 2011:

Two tour operators were by yesterday still missing after the boat they were using for a familiarisation tour of Chobe Lodge, capsized on River Nile in Murchison Falls National Park, Nwoya District, on Saturday. Speaking at a press conference in Kampala yesterday, Trade and Tourism Minister Kahinda Otafiire said about 30 operators took boat rides in shifts but the last group, which left at about 6 PM had not returned by the expected time of 7 PM.

One of those tour operators was Cliff. The other was a Mrs. Jalia Mujtebi. After a month of searching neither body had been recovered. Thanks to the phalanx of crocodiles that lined the Nile below the Falls, I suspect they never will.

Cliff left behind a wife and four daughters and a custom safari business that was on the verge of stardom. He was the preferred guide for *Save the Children*, Jane Goodall and Disney. He was responsible for introducing a rhino to a new park in Uganda to mate with a Kenyan rhino and thus help reintroduce rhinos to Uganda. He had been working with the BBC and Disney World to produce a film about

Cliff Kisitu, tour guide at Murchison Falls, Uganda, four years before he accidentally drowned here.

chimpanzees. He was going to appear in the film. In other words the world was about to learn what I had learned at first hand when Cliff coaxed the school children into singing "I am the youngest star."

There is a picture at the end of this book of two guides, one on either side of me beneath a sign that says Equator. The guide on the right is Ben Musisi. Cliff is on the left, the man with his hand close to my heart. We are singing an African folk song that Cliff taught me. The lyrics are:

Jambo
Hello.
Jambo bwana
Hello, sir.
Habari gani?
How are you?
Mzuri sana
Very well.
Wageni wakaribishwa
Foreigners, you are welcome.
Uganda yetu
In our Uganda
Hakuna matata
There is no problem.

We ad-libbed our own ending, a call and response.

How are you Ben?
Ben has no problem.

How are you Cliff?
Cliff has no problem.
How are you, Jay?
Jay has no problem

Cliff's last e-mail to me, sent five years after we first met in Uganda read:

Hullo my Dear Friend Jay OLYOTYA SSEBO OLI BULUNGI? I miss you so much and all the girls are sending their greetings to you. Sherry has joined University remember she wanted to be a Teacher now she joined Tourism she is doing Bachelor in Tourism at the university.

Here I had been fretting all these years about Africa killing me. In the end it was one of her own that she took.

CHAPTER 9

❧ ❦

Signposts

Street lamps in Rome near Piazza Navona.

As I think back over the memories that travel has pasted in my mental album, I realize that they were all in their way sign posts, fingers pointing to the answer to my puzzle: Why do I force myself to follow Nancy everywhere in her traveling world even though the thought of it fills me with anxiety? One such memory involved a visit to the church of San Martino ai Monte in Rome. It stands atop a 4th century Roman household, a so-called titulus, a house-church of early Rome. Its owner, Equitius, used his dwelling as a meeting-place now that, thanks to Constantine, Christians were allowed to congregate openly. An actual church was built on the site of Equitius' home by order of Pope Sylvester I (reigned 314–335), a pope whose life was so uneventful that miraculous events had to be invented for him to warrant his elevation to sainthood. For example, it was said of Sylvester that he cured Constantine of leprosy, a disease that, in fact, he never had.

There was method in the magic. *The Donation of Constantine* was a late 8th or early 9th century document of unknown authorship claiming that Constantine had given to Sylvester—and, in fact, to all subsequent popes—spiritual dominion throughout the Holy Roman Empire but, more importantly, political authority over Rome and western Europe. It was a tremendous gift and one that was terribly useful to subsequent papal generations. What caused

I MARRIED A TRAVEL JUNKIE

Constantine to give away a significant portion of his dominion? Gratitude, of course. Sylvester I had cured his leprosy.

An anonymous author, probably a Lateran cleric, exploited that myth in a document conferring power and realm on the church. *The Donation of Constantine* took a hundred years to sink in, but when it did, it did with a vengeance. It was cited as authority in the fateful schism of 1054 when Cardinal Humbert placed the papal bull of excommunication on the altar of Hagia Sophia in Constantinople, leading to the split between East and West that has lasted right up through today.

Five hundred years after the schism, Pope Eugenius IV, at war with Alphonso of Aragon, King of Naples, attempted to use *The Donation* as a legitimizing authority for his war. To retaliate Alphonso employed the services of the medieval Italian polemicist and philosopher, Lorenzo Valla (1407–1457). In 1440 Valla wrote a document called *The Declamatio.* In it he showed conclusively that the 400-year-old *Donation of Constantine* was a forgery. Valla argued that the crude Latin of *The Donation* was completely out of step with the Latin of Sylvester's time, using inappropriate words like *banna* instead of *vexillum* for "flag," or *clericare* for "ordain."

Valla's debunking, a valiant effort, had little effect. Four hundred years after having been shown to be a sham, the Papacy continued to invoke its authority. Those familiar with contemporary uses of *The Protocols of the Learned Elders of Zion* will not be surprised.

All of this resonated as I entered San Martino ai Monte, a building that was begun in the 4th century and achieved its current incarnation in the mid-17th century. It was a reminder of how long-lived a sham can be. As we entered the church a group of school children disappeared down a set of stairs at the far end of the nave. We followed them and found ourselves descending into the depths of San Martino. Soon we had left the children well behind us and were still able to go deeper and deeper into the depths of the church.

The sub-sub-basement was dank and dark. The floors were dirt, the ceilings extraordinarily high. At the bottom, or what I thought was the bottom, I saw yet one more level. It was completely dark down there. No bare light bulb hanging from a single cord to relieve the blackness, just a grave-sized opening into a large cavernous gloom. I had been mindful that as we went down each flight of stone steps, we were sinking back in time—first to Valla's *Declamatio* of 1440 and then to the anonymous *Donation of Constantine* itself, sometime between 750 and 800. Having come this far, I wanted to go all the way. Nancy said she would wait for me. I started down the final flight of steps toward the time of the original titulus, Equitius' house itself, 300 AD. Halfway down I felt a cold chill. Whether it came from the darkness in front of me or the darkness inside me, I don't know. All I know is I wasn't going any further. I turned around and scurried back up the steps to where Nancy was standing.

"Why did you stop?" she asked.

"I'm not sure," I said.

It was true. I wasn't sure. But it had something to do with Nancy not being there with me. It had to do with my feeling, for a fleeting instant, of being completely alone. I didn't like that feeling, not one bit.

San Martino ai Monte wasn't the first time I'd felt like that. We had visited San Martino in the spring of 2005. Some ten years earlier when we were in Tanzania, Nancy and I were visiting a rock, Kisima Rock. It is located in the Maasai steppes of Tanzania. Kisima Rock is a huge stone slab, maybe five or six acres across. It is surrounded by an unremitting savannah that recedes into the distance as far as the eye can see, an endless plain dotted with spiny-thorn commifera, chicken-foot grass, and, the one extravagance in a sea of sameness, the baobab tree—a giant up close, but dwarfed by the landscape it was growing in.

In the middle of Kisima Rock is a bowl-shaped indentation, 20 feet across, 15 feet deep. It is almost perfectly round and the edges are smooth, as if some imaginary faucet had been dripping onto it for the past million years. Since Kisima Rock itself is the highest point around, there is no place for water to fall from. How, then, did Nature fashion it? Maybe some softer stone, round as a melon, had been embedded in it. The passage of countless rainstorms may have melted the melon stone, leaving its imprint behind. Who knows? In America, say in the Badlands of South Dakota, this natural wonder would have merited a special name. There would have been a sign shaped like a pointing finger. Burned into it would be a legend, something like "The Devil's Drinking Cup" or "Satan's Sink." Here nothing marked its presence, a throwaway of a natural wonder.

On this particular day seven of us lunched on the rock. Afterwards my companions went in search of a tribe of baboons they had spotted earlier. I stayed behind to write my journal. I had an unobstructed 360° view. Everywhere I looked was an immensity of sameness. The sky was robin egg blue. Cotton ball clouds impelled by a steady wind floated slowly by. Engrossed in my journal, I hadn't realized that everyone had gone. I happened to look up. I was alone, a thousand miles from anywhere I knew. I scanned the vastness for signs of life. Nothing. Just the movement of the wind past my ears. In that dreadful moment, before I mercifully caught sight of my companions coming back up over the rim of a nearby ridge, I was aware of a sensation I have never felt before, that of being utterly and completely alone.

Michel Peissel, a far more intrepid explorer than I will ever be, describes a similar moment in his 1967 book, *The Kingdom of Mustang*. He had reached a village called Namdral in northern Nepal. Tibet was a few thousand yards away. Just outside the village he looked south toward the gigantic Annapurna and Dhaulagiri mountain ranges. From his vantage point they appeared to be floating somewhere below him.

The most indescribable beauty stretching around me was of a grandeur that spoke to the soul and fulfilled my wildest dreams. It was only the barking of a dog that brought me back to reality, and the result was that with the howling wind that flogged against me I became filled with a sense of solitude that recalled depressing thoughts. Perhaps I would never see again the seemingly unreal world of my past; I might never be able to bear witness to this panorama that I had been given the pleasure of contemplating.

Peissel was pained that he might never be able to share the moment with others. For me sharing that particular moment would have been like kissing someone when you had a sore throat.

This business of travelers suddenly finding themselves overwhelmed by loneliness is not all that uncommon. In Tony Horwitz' *Blue Latitudes*, he describes a walk he took into Waipi'o Valley at the north end of the island of Hawaii. He was retracing the steps of Captain James Cook. The valley was of interest because of the many rumors circulating that Cook's bones were buried in caves in the cliffs above the valley floor. This is how he described his visit:

> A steady rain pelted down. The valley before me looked jungly, the way I imagined the Mekong Delta or an Amazonian rain forest: swamped paddies, huge-fronded palms, trees dripping with rain and fruit, the whole scene so green it seemed to vibrate. More than at any moment in my Pacific travels, I suddenly felt very far away, alone in a landscape utterly foreign to me.

History is filled with stories of human beings finding themselves in a land or seascape that has no place for them. I think of Ernest Shackleton's incredible escape from Antarctica. Leaving most of his men on Elephant Island, he set out in a small boat to cross the evil expanse of the Southern Ocean. His destination was South Georgia Island. He was a third of the way across when a storm blew up. *The Caird* and its tiny crew fought mountainous seas urged up by a three-day-running, 60-knot gale. The temperature was below zero. Ice had begun to collect on every surface forcing the boat deeper and deeper into the sea like a coffin being lowered into its grave.

Chipping away at the ice to restore buoyancy, the crew was near their breaking point when, suddenly out of nowhere, a lone albatross appeared. It hovered a mere ten feet over their heads. Then, on its 11-foot wingspan, it soared in a matter of seconds several hundred feet up, only to drop down again like a child on a sliding board. The men in the skiff watched with what I imagine must have been a mélange of envy, awe, and anger as the creature flew above them hour after hour with the utmost elegance and grace. What was, for them, a gale of life-threatening proportions was, for the albatross, a playground.

How often I have felt, when I travel, as if I were in a world whose inhabitants are as naturally wedded to their place as a leaf to a tree, a world in which I am as out of place as a mermaid on a treadmill. I felt this way in Australia. Driving to see Ormiston Gorge about 135 kilometers west of Alice Springs, I was on a dirt road that cut through central Australia's semi-arid desert. Friends in Alice Springs had loaned me their pickup truck to make the trip. They warned me that if I were to wander off the road and not find my way back, the desert would claim me in 16 hours flat. The farther away from Alice Springs I drove, the more anxious I became. I found it hard to see where the road stopped and the desert began. For all I knew, I was already off the road. I must have been doing 40 miles an hour when all of a sudden a kangaroo came bounding out of nowhere. I jammed on the brakes. He missed me by no more than six inches. Had I hit him at that speed, the truck would have been totaled. And I as well, if not from the impact, then from an environment that might as well have been on Mars.

Why did that kangaroo chose my pickup to run in front of? Was it some kind of kamikaze impulse? Did he think I was another kangaroo? Whatever it was, the experience made me realize how thin the boundary is between my world and the ones I travel in. The kangaroo almost succeeded in pushing me out of my world into his.

CHAPTER 10

❧ ❧

Why Travel?

Chinese photography club members photographing Nancy
photographing them at the Xihai (West Sea) Grand Canyon scenic
area in the Huangshan (Yellow) Mountains, Anhui Province, China.

The average traveler when asked why he or she travels almost always responds with something like, "I want to experience someone else's culture." That's a red herring. How can you experience someone else's culture from an air-conditioned bus going 20 miles an hour through the streets of Pusan? All right. Get off the bus and walk through the fish market. You haven't experienced someone else's culture. All you've experienced is a lot of fish for sale. Most anthropologists spend years trying to get inside someone else's culture. Many of them come back home to a nervous breakdown for their efforts. Culture hopping isn't easy.

Or again, travelers will tell you they travel to see something new and interesting, something spectacular. That's probably true. But don't take that at face value either. Why do people want to see something spectacular—the terraced rice paddies of Bali that look like green wedding cakes, the temples of Angkor Wat that look like a Macy's Thanksgiving Day Parade in the middle of the jungle, the fjords of New Zealand's South Island that look like a scene from *The Lord of the Rings,* which, in fact, they are? You don't need to travel to see something spectacular. Wherever you are, there is something spectacular. I don't care if you are within shouting distance of the Trenton, New Jersey, oil refineries or the Fresh Kills Landfill, the garbage island that for 50 years—until it was closed on July 4, 2001—received its daily ration of trash from the City of New York. Anything seen for the first time is spectacular. Even the house you live in. I mean if you really look hard.

The problem is repetition. Seeing something spectacular over and over is like attaching barnacle after barnacle to the hull of a ship. Sooner or later it becomes so encrusted it sinks to the bottom of the sea of memories. That's why a lot of people travel: to re-experience the feeling of seeing something spectacular for the first time, even if it was their own toes in their own crib. It isn't contempt that familiarity breeds. It's indifference. Travelers are running away from indifference.

This insensitivity to the spectacular has sometimes been laid at the door of lack of imagination. For example, in *Siren Wind* Norman Douglas accuses the Italians of being blind to the beauty around them, a blindness arising from an excess of realism. For them the turquoise waters of the Mediterranean are a source of fish, the silvery leaves of the olive trees merely a source of olives.

It is an unfair criticism. Unlike the locals, travelers are not saddled with the burden, day after day after day, of seeing a remarkable cathedral surrounded by towering mountains, or a picturesque cloister perched atop a far off peak. No one can do that and still retain the freshness of the first glimpse. Immediacy fades as quickly as an echo. In fact, it is just because the experience is fleeting that the moments travelers live for are possible.

Every so often I hear someone say how wonderful it would

be to live in Segesta for a year, to be able to see that incredible temple every day. Be careful what you wish for. How many times can you look at a temple before it becomes the New Jersey Turnpike?

The earth-worker and essayist, Robert Smithson, understood this. In his 1967 paean to the flotsam and jetsam of an industrial state, *A Tour of the Monuments of Passaic, New Jersey*, he asked, "Has Passaic replaced Rome as the Eternal City?"

My answer is, "Fat chance. Bobby."

Even so he was on to something important—the spectacular in anything seen for the first time.

So maybe travelers travel for the sake of that first moment, the one that passes as soon as it comes, like the click of a camera's shutter. That, too, is an old tape running, the one that says avoid boredom at all costs. Give me novelty or give me death.

I suppose Paul Theroux is this generation's most widely read and respected travel writer. In his book *The Happy Isles of Oceania*, this is what he has to say about why one (he) travels:

Travel, which is nearly always seen as an attempt to escape from the ego, is in my opinion the opposite. Nothing induces concentration or inspires memory like an alien landscape or a foreign culture. It is simply not possible (as romantics think) to lose yourself in an exotic place. Much more likely is an experience of intense nostalgia, a harking back to an earlier stage of your life, or seeing clearly a serious mistake. But this does not happen to the exclusion of the exotic present. What makes the whole experience vivid, and sometimes thrilling, is the juxtaposition of the present and the past—London seen from the heights of Harris Saddle.

In other words people travel to (re-)capture an intense nostalgia for the past, a nostalgia that brings with it the special frisson of remembering the past in an exotic present. For some people this is undoubtedly true. I know someone who grew up in the wilds of Louisiana. He never left the sticks until he went to college. Being a very bright boy, he went to a very good college. But before then, the only traveling he did was to the movie house in the center of his one-movie-house town. He saw images of Athens, Rome, and Paris. Later thanks to a college education and a good job, he traveled to those places. When he got there he was overwhelmed by a sense of longing for the place where he'd first glimpsed those cities—the movie house in the sticks.

Satchel Paige, with whom I share the same birthday—July 7—famously said, "Don't look back. Something might be gaining on you." I'm with Paige. That's why the Theroux moment doesn't work for me. I am as blind to nostalgia as a dog is to the color red.

My lack of interest extends to the family homestead. I have no interest in traveling to Minsk, the town in Byelorussia where my father was born, the town his family had escaped from when they came to America in 1903. What in the world would I see? Bricks and mortar? Sticks and stones? I have friends who have executed "a return" to the ancestral home in Poland. They have sought out the street, the house, even the apartment their parents grew up in. They knocked on the door. They were invited in. They came home filled with emotion. They couldn't tell me why. I didn't want to probe. It would have been disrespectful. In the anonymity of these pages I can ask: What did they expect would happen once they stepped inside those repainted, re-papered, re-peopled walls? Did they think long dead Uncle Shike would suddenly appear in a hologram from the other side, that he would apologize for rebuking them because they ate a cookie before sundown on Yom Kippur?

When Gertrude Stein returned to Oakland only to find her family home gone, she said, "There's no there there."

I'll buy that. When you're gone, the family home is gone as well. Even when it's not.

So we're back to the same question. Why do I travel? I've assured myself in the past that it's because Nancy does. But there's more to it than that. I am not just a good guy, someone willing to put his anxieties on the backburner to uphold his marital vows. The truth is that I travel because I don't want to be left behind. This is not a new feeling, one that Nancy had nothing to do with.

I used to take my son camping every summer from the time he was ten years old. We would go out for two weeks at a time. I did it because it seemed like the fatherly thing to do. It must have been hell on him. My travel anxiety manifested itself even then.

Whenever we set up tent in some backwoods campground,

I MARRIED A TRAVEL JUNKIE

I worried that some bearded guy in a woolen cap and a plaid shirt was waiting, ax in hand, until we dozed off. I would lie awake at night, staring at the canvas ceiling listening for that telltale crack of a twig. One summer in a desperate attempt to avoid death by axes I took $700 out of the bank—the amount I normally set aside for these trips—and offered the money to Ben. "This is yours," I said, "if we stay home this year." I did not have Nancy's scruples. I was not above bribing my own son. Ben refused. My bad. Good for him.

One summer my daughter Beth complained that I only went camping with her brother. She was 16 years old. Ben, two years her junior, jumped at the idea of Beth coming along. I thought it was because he loved his sister. While that was undoubtedly true and—I'm happy to say—remains so to this day, the truth of that summer lay elsewhere. He wanted his sister along as a buffer between us. No one ever travels for travel's sake. There is always an ulterior motive.

On this particular trip the three of us went to the Laurentian Mountains in Quebec Province. One day we stayed at a campground that had a tranquil river flowing through it and canoes for the borrowing. My children decided to paddle up the river. They insisted on going alone. I can't say I blamed them. I watched them disappear around a bend. As soon as they were out of sight, I was out of my mind. What if something happened to them? Maybe there were rapids? A bear could be fishing in the stream and, absent salmon, fixate on them. I knew the last thing in the world they wanted was for me to follow them. It was crystal clear to me that I should leave them alone. This was an important moment in their lives. They wanted to be free of me, to be with one another and to demonstrate that they could handle the world. I told myself all that. But it was useless. I grabbed the nearest canoe and scuttled after them.

When I caught up to them, Beth saw that I was sitting legs crossed in the bottom of the canoe. From the point of view of stability, it was apparently the worst possible place to sit. (What did I know?) She worried that if the canoe capsized, I (and they) would be in trouble. She instructed me on the proper way to sit in a canoe. Then, the three of us paddled— they sullenly, me, sheepishly—back to camp. We were all on a rescue mission, in this instance trying to save one another.

I once would have said that I run after Nancy the way I ran after my children: to protect her. Maybe I am driven to stay close to Nancy by the anxiety of living in a dangerous world. Maybe lurking behind every potted palm in every hotel lobby I'll ever cross I expect to find twins and a packet of matches. Maybe I want to protect her from those twins.

Naaaaaah. I don't think so. As my old shrink would have said, "Dig deeper."

O.K. I'll dig a little deeper.

I was with her the night my mother died. The hospital called at 11 PM. They thought I'd better come down. She was in intensive care after an operation to repair a broken hip. The strain of the operation proved too much. She had a heart attack. The doctors were keeping her alive with tubes and monitors and drugs. I'd actually been in the room when the heart attack struck. The nurses and their aides rushed in with a gurney and wheeled her away. We had been talking. She complained of chest pains. I called the nurse and in an instant I was marginalized. A doctor came back to her room to find me. She told me my mother had been stabilized and that I should go home. They would call me if they needed me. At 11 PM that night they needed me. All the doctor would say was, "I think it would be a good idea if you came down."

My son, Benjamin, came with me. He was 21 years old and had the bad luck to be home when I got the call. We were led into the intensive care unit. Everything was dark except the bed in the far corner of the vast, equipment filled room. My mother lay trussed like a Thanksgiving turkey, tubes rising out of her like columns of smoke. The death scene was short. My mother looked at me. There was recognition in her eyes. Then she rolled her eyes toward the ceiling. The heart monitor flat-lined. That was that.

Benjamin told me he didn't know what was happening. It all happened so quickly. He remembers a hospital staffer whispering to him that she was going and that now was the time to say goodbye. Nobody whispered to me. I stood there and watched her slip away. I began to run around in circles the way my dog, Tuppence, did just before she died. When I got hold of myself, my first thought was appropriate for a ten year old, not a 51-year-old.

"How could you possibly choose death over me?"

In other words like a child it was all about me. My mother was my only surviving parent. Now she was gone. In that moment the numbing reality of what death is all about hit me. My mother doted on me. Everything I ever did was food for prideful gossip with her friends; my scholarships, my faculty appointments, my publications, my awards. All of that she hoarded like a miser hoarding gold, opening the treasure chest to show her friends before slamming it shut again. But that night I learned that there was something stronger even than my mother's unbending love for me.

CHAPTER 11

~❧ ❧~

What's It All About, Nancy?

Taktsang Monastery (Tiger's Nest) in the upper
Paro Valley, Bhutan, where the author was unable
to follow his wife, Nancy.

So here we are at the nexus, the nub, the knot. Thanks to my mother and that gorilla who told me to back off or she would break my back, I've learned where the edges are. I have learned the most important lesson there is: I am a separate person. So is the person closest to my heart, Nancy. We each have our boundaries. No matter how much we might care for one another, those boundaries are uncrossable. They are like a Berlin Wall that won't—in fact, ought not—come down.

Following Nancy around the world like a trained seal wasn't going to change that truth, try as I might to think otherwise. And it was a small but potent list of travel memories that seem to matter more than the others, memories that were somehow marked with a footnote that said, "Pay special attention. There is more here than just the memory."

First on the list was that visit to San Martino ai Monte in Rome, the one where I went deeper and deeper into the subbasements of the church, leaving Nancy farther and farther behind until, as if an ice-cold, iron hand had caught hold of the back of my neck, I could go no further and rushed back up the steps to join her.

The second memory was of that gorilla in the Bwindi Impenetrable Forest, the one who showed me what boundaries meant and why it was important not to cross them.

The third was an encounter with an elephant in the

Moremi game preserve in Botswana in 2000. He was very old, maybe 55 years. His skin hung around him like drapery. His eyelashes had grown so long they covered his eyes like a veil. His tusks were the color of earth, turned brown after decades of gouging trees for bark and plowing the ground for minerals. He had given up any desire to clean them. Although the ground was strewn with a variety of elephant fodder, he selected just one—the tender morning glory vine.

Our guide on this trip—his name was Jeff—had maneuvered the Land Cruiser within 25 feet of the elephant. I watched him eat, methodically, mechanically, as if he were doing it out of habit rather than need. He was still a huge if ancient bull. His ears were ragged, both pierced by something the size of a bullet. Despite his bulk I was not intimidated. It was clear he had encountered the likes of us many times. There was not even a hint of challenge.

"How much longer does he have?" I asked Jeff.

"Maybe 15 years."

"How will he die?"

Jeff said that first he would begin to lose the last of his six sets of teeth. Then he would go to the river where he would chew the thin, soft plants of the river's banks and bottom. When his teeth were gone completely, he would starve to death.

"Between now and then, will he rejoin a herd?"

"Most likely he has had enough of that life," Jeff said. "Now he wants to be alone. We are a nuisance he knows will go away soon enough and leave him be."

This was our last game drive in Botswana. On the way

back to camp—it had already grown dark—Jeff asked me, "Do you really not like Africa? There must be something that you will take away with you."

I answered there was something terribly sad about that bull elephant.

He said, "Then you get it. You understand about Africa."

Perhaps I understood about Africa. More to the point, I began to understand about myself—that my desire to follow Nancy around the world was not a selfless act. Rather, it was born of pure selfishness. By following her, I was hoping the distance between us would disappear completely. In other words, I was hoping to make her me. Each of these memories was a signpost pointing in the opposite direction: I am only me. Nancy is only her. Let her travel if she wants. Let me travel if I want, not because she wants. I have regurgitated this now-we-are-one nonsense. How perfectly detrimental that must be to healthy unions. Much better for the preacher to say, "Now you are separate. Help one another make it through whatever this is."

My own special brand of travel neurosis revolved around my not wanting to acknowledge that simple fact of human existence. That's why I ran after my children. They were going to leave me alone in a backwoods campground. That's why I ran around in circles when my mother died. That's why I ran after Nancy. They were all trying to teach me a lesson I wasn't ready to learn. Ironic that travel should have done the trick for me. As St. Augustine said, "...people travel to marvel at the mountains, seas, rivers and stars; and they pass right by themselves without astonishment."

There was one more memory, the most recent one. It was also the least subtle. Even so I didn't quite get it when it happened. I was getting closer to confronting this business of the self and the significant other. It just took awhile to sink in.

It happened on May 24, 2007, an auspicious day, as the Buddhists might say. It was the day after Nancy and I first went out together some 17 years earlier. It was an anniversary of sorts, an anniversary of a new beginning. We were, of all places, in Bhutan, the one country I actively wanted to visit—outside of Italy, that is. The fourth king of Bhutan, His Majesty Jigme Singye Wangchuck, had decided that the recipe for Bhutan's Gross Domestic Product, the GDP, was missing an important ingredient: the happiness of the people. From the mid-1980's on he sponsored conferences, seminars, discussions, and books, all aimed at trying to define happiness and fold it into a quantifiable portrait of Bhutan. Two years before our visit Gross National Happiness as a national goal had been written into the constitution. I wanted to see for myself the country that had put happiness on the front burner.

The visit didn't begin happily. The approach to the country's only airport in Paro was hair-raising. When the captain announced the descent, all I could see was an unending field of clouds and, in the far distance, the peak of an enormous mountain jutting up through it. This was Kanchenjunga. At 29,169 feet it is the third highest mountain in the world. It sank in that I was in a different part of the world, a part where Earth and Sky, at least that portion of the sky I was accustomed to flying in, met. The plane dove into the clouds.

Kanchenjunga disappeared. When we emerged, the captain advised us not to be alarmed if the plane appeared to be close to the mountains on either side of the aircraft. That was putting it mildly. It seemed as if the wings would clip the tops off the blue pine trees racing by. Then, just as suddenly, the plane straightened, dove again, and we were on the ground in Paro.

We drove straight to the capital, Thimphu, a 40-mile trip that took four hours. Bhutan is a small country, just 800 square miles—smaller, in fact, than Vermont and New Hampshire combined. From East to West there is only one road, the lateral highway. It is a little over 150 miles long. The Indian government built it in 1960 using Indian laborers. When Nancy and I arrived almost 50 years later, Indian laborers were widening it for the 2008 coronation of the fifth king.

The road was a nightmare. Pockmarked by potholes, it was an asphalt strip barely able to handle two compact cars abreast. Because roadwork was in full swing, private vehicles were restricted to certain hours of the day. We chose the 3:30 PM to 4:30 PM window. Apparently, everyone else did as well. Huge trucks, small vans, busses and motorcycles, all jostled one another for position. As we stumbled along, traffic jams constantly jolted us to a halt while drivers negotiated the tight squeeze they had gotten into. These generally occurred at a bend in the road where the shoulders were the narrowest. The vehicles edged past one another with less than an inch of clearance. The drivers took this in stride. No tempers flared. No angry words exchanged. It was just the cost of doing business in Bhutan.

The road ran along the edge of a precipice that dropped

off into the cultivated fields alongside the Paro River several hundred feet below. Cars coming in the opposite direction nudged us onto the shoulder. Dust and dirt swirled. We were either winding the van's windows up to keep grime out or down to let air in. Along the roadside migrant Indian workers, like an endless prison gang, broke large rocks into smaller ones. The hammers they used were a function of the size of the men and women wielding them. Small children played nearby while their parents hacked away or shoveled. The shovelers often worked in pairs. One would hold the shovel close to the ground while a second yanked on a rope tied just above the blade. The motion drew the blade deep into whatever pile—dirt, stone, or trash—had to be moved. Presumably this made it easier for the shoveler. All she had to do was lift and carry. Every so often we passed neat piles of stone assorted by size ready for a nearby section of the roadbed.

The Buddhists have a vision of six levels of existence, each level represented by a syllable in the sacred chant: *O mani padme om.* The lowest level is the "hell of hells." The Indian workers along the road were surely living at the level of *om.* We passed shantytowns made of tarpaper and tin, scraps of wood, sheets of paper, all shoehorned into creases in the mountainsides or along ledges just feet from the roadway and its incessant dust. As bad as these conditions were, I imagined that they were an improvement over what the workers faced back home. Still it seemed that these people were living in a prison without walls. We passed one woman thin as a rail standing ramrod straight amid the banging of mallet against stone and the clouds of dirty, dust-soaked air. She was suckling an infant. This was her baby's nursery. I doubted the fourth king's efforts to define happiness included the migrant workers who were widening the road for his son's coronation.

Bhutan is a country of mountains and prayer flags. It rises from a height of 500 feet above sea level in the south to close to 25,000 feet above sea level in the north. It does all this rising in 100 miles, roughly the distance from Boston to New Haven, Connecticut. Gangkhar Puensum, at 24,836 feet, is Bhutan's highest mountain. It is, in fact, the highest unclimbed mountain in the world. Unclimbed it will remain. To the Bhutanese it is a sacred mountain that must not be defiled.

The Bhutanese believe that the higher up you are the purer you are. Prayer flags fly from 25-foot poles on mountain ridges that seem completely inaccessible. How anyone climbed up there, let alone carried all those poles with them—the poles are often in groups of 29—is beyond me. But there they are, white flags with *O mani padme om* printed on them, snapping in the high winds that play at those heights like Shelley's *Spirit fierce* in his *Ode to the West Wind*. The wind gives voice to the prayer. Literally borne on a breeze, the prayers make their way to the gods.

The snapping of prayer flags, the ringing of bells set in motion by prayer wheels—themselves set in motion by a mountain stream or the sheer man- or womanpower of someone turning a wheel in a public square or at the entrance to a monastery—has turned Bhutan into one gigantic wind chime.

One day Nancy and I started out to visit Takshang Monastery. The monastery was perched high up on a mountain at the edge of a cliff that dropped 2,600 feet to the valley floor. The monastery is the most sacred in all of the Himalayas. In the 8th century Guru Rinpoche, the second Buddha, meditated for three months in a cave here in order to bring Buddhism to Paro Valley. A sanctuary of one kind or another has existed on the spot for the past 700 years. The monastery is built around that cave. According to Buddhist tradition, Guru Rinpoche came on the back of one of his consorts. She assumed the shape of a flying tigress for the journey. Takshang means "tiger's nest."

The walk to the monastery is in three stages. The first is to a teahouse. It takes an hour to reach it if, like Nancy and me, you are not used to the thin air that turns moderately difficult ascents into sheer travail. From the teahouse we looked straight across a craggy valley to the monastery. We were at 9,700 feet, having dragged ourselves 1,000 feet up the mountainside from the road below.

The teahouse view is mind-boggling. The monastery is a white-walled, wooden-roofed, many-windowed fantasy that seems to be growing up out of the cliff rock along with the blue pine trees that surround it. The steps leading up are well hidden. This heightens the sense of isolation and inaccessibility that hovers over the building like a halo. Hidden away in a crevice just below the monastery is a much smaller building, a meditation hall. Here monks come to meditate for three years, three months, and three days. When we reached the teahouse, it was rumored that a monk was inside the hall this very minute. Food was slipped under the door. He communicated his needs by scribbling on a piece of paper and leaving it on the doorstep outside, all this so that he might not come in contact with another human being for the period of his self-imposed isolation. I tried to imagine him sitting cross-legged inside, a long scraggly beard resting on his knees, his hair falling in unkempt tangles to his shoulders, his eyes shining despite the dimness of the light in the room, seeing absolutely nothing except what was going on inside his head. He is what the Tibetans call "a living ghost."

The second stage of the walk to the monastery is 800 feet higher up, 800 additional feet of steep climbing. It takes you to a spot well above the Takshang Monastery. If from here you want to go all the way to the monastery itself, you must climb down a steep set of steps carved into the side of the mountain, cross a tiny stream that sprang to life when Yeshe Tshogyel, one of Guru Rinpoche's wives, threw her rosary against the rocks, and then climb up another set of steps to the monastery proper.

At the teahouse Nancy and I parted company though I, at least, didn't mean to. Climbing to 9,700 feet had been extremely debilitating for me. I had underestimated how enervating lack of oxygen could be. For the last hundred or so steps to the teahouse, I felt as if I were dragging a ball and chain. I collapsed into a chair beneath an umbrella set out on the teahouse veranda. I could go no farther. I was sure Nancy couldn't either. I underestimated her. When the guide announced that he was leaving for the second stage, Nancy said she was going.

I remembered my wedding vow: Whither thou goest, I go. But I literally could not move. It was as if I were wedded to

Nancy but welded to that chair. She knew I wanted to go with her. But she also knew that I was running on empty. She had a choice. Go on or stay with me.

"I'm only going to the second stage," she promised.

It was safari fever and the Engaruka Plain all over again. I shouldn't have been surprised. I was too spent to argue. I watched helplessly as she disappeared up the path. I sat there as if I were mired in quicksand. One half hour later, through my binoculars, I saw her emerge at the second lookout point. She was moving about taking photographs. Occasionally she would disappear behind a thicket. She would re-emerge. Then I saw her descending the stairway that led to Tiger's Nest itself. She seemed tentative, as if she were just testing the stairway. About 20 steps down she stopped, looked up, and waved in my direction. She couldn't possibly have seen me from that distance. Even so she must have sensed that I would be watching her through the binoculars. She must have made a decision at just that moment. She looked in my direction as if to confirm it. She took a few more steps down. Then she dropped completely out of sight.

More time passed, maybe 45 minutes. I kept scanning the second lookout point and the steps that went down and then up to the monastery. No Nancy. I held off going into the teahouse for lunch. She'll be coming down the path any minute, I thought. Then, something told me to train my binoculars on Tiger's Nest. The instant I did I saw her emerge from the darkness of a corridor onto a veranda of the monastery proper. I saw her look down into the 2,600-foot abyss. I watched as she sank back into the darkness of the corridor behind her. The whole thing lasted no more than 30 seconds, a minute at the most. Yet, somehow, her appearance on that veranda and the lifting of my binoculars had been perfectly timed by the two of us. It was as if we were connected, even though a 2,600-foot valley separated us. The lesson in that was about to dawn on me.

Nancy had gone all the way to the Tiger's Nest. I was furious. How could she go there without me? She said she was coming right back. If I'd known she was going all the way, I would have made a superhuman effort to go with her. I only stayed in that chair because she said she'd be right back.

My anger took me by surprise. What's going on? I wondered. Why am I angry? How could I possibly expect her not to go there? Here we both were, just a few thousand feet away from the most sacred monastery in Bhutan, itself half-way around the world from home. Here she was a woman consumed by the need to travel to strange and exotic places. What could be stranger or more exotic than a monastery perched on a 2,600-foot-high cliff just above a tiny house where a monk had cloistered himself for three years, three months, and three days? When would either of us come this way again? Could I really expect her to stay with me when she had the energy to climb and I didn't?

Then it hit me. Nancy's climb to Tiger's Nest was a replay of my mother's death. Both were exercises in separation. It was intensive care all over again. I was being left behind. As soon as that realization sprang to mind, my anger subsided. That's how psychotherapy works. At least, that's how my auto-psychotherapy works. All the angst I suffer—all the pain, the fear, the sweaty palms—all that comes down to namelessness. But put a name to the fear and damn if the fear doesn't metamorphose into something much less, well, fearful.

The bullet isn't all magic. If it were, I suppose I'd say, the next time Nancy proposes a trip to Antarctica, or Papua New Guinea or the Seychelles, "Sure, sweetheart. You go right along. Have fun. Drop me a post card. I'll pick you up at the airport when you get back."

Perhaps I'll say that. I doubt it. It is one thing to know what is going on. It is quite another to change it. I will probably continue to travel with Nancy as long as she is up to it.

55 year old elephant in the Moremi Game Preserve, Botswana, living out the remainder of his life apart from a herd.

She loves it. And it is the screen on which I write the history of the world. It is for me a teacher. So what if it is difficult. Lord knows learning isn't easy.

That is the least of it. The important thing is that now I know about the distance between Nancy and me—a short distance, certainly, but a distance nonetheless. I think of it as a kind of no-man's-land, one that I tried to pretend never existed, and then when I came to realize that it did, one I tried to cross. I suppose the wisdom that I have gleaned from travel is this: let the distance between yourself and the one you love be. There is nothing you can do about it. That is just the way things are. There is, of course, a flip side: no matter how hard you try, you are in the end alone.

Epilogue

～❦～

Nancy has always said I protest too much. She says I couldn't possibly be as anxious about travel as I claim to. I have too good a time when I'm wherever she takes me. She says she wouldn't dream of putting me through the hell I say I am going through if she thought for one minute I was really going through it. She doesn't mean she would stay at home. She means she would insist I stay at home.

Nancy says I'm a good traveler, even better than that. She points to my trying to learn the language of whatever country or region we are in and that I go out of my way to try to talk to the locals in their language. That's true. I have teach-yourself books on Swahili, Arabic, Japanese, Italian, Vietnamese, Maori, and Bahasa Indonesian on my bookshelf. After all, I am a linguist by trade. I find it fun hammering away at the language du jour for a couple of weeks. When a group we were hosting visited a marae in New Zealand, I surprised the hell out of the Maori by delivering a welcome speech in their language. I had help from a Maori-speaking friend. But, even so, I got a kick out of that. I admit it.

I suppose you could say that if I really were that stressed, I wouldn't give a thought to the local language. That isn't true. I have learned over the years, to use my shrink's language, to externalize pain. In common parlance that translates as: if life hands you a lemon, make lemonade.

Once I am committed to a trip, I have learned to make the best of it. Horses, I'm told, kick and scream when they get caught in a barbed-wire fence. Mules, on the other hand, quietly wait for help. By that criterion I'm with the asses. I read as much as I can about the places we're going to before we go there. I write journals while I'm there. I rethink what I know

about the world when I get back. When it comes to knowing the dimensions of the world I live in, I am a much better educated person now than I was when I met Nancy 20 years ago. I hereby acknowledge that debt.

I asked Nancy if she had changed as a result of our relationship. She told me she had. She said that before we met she was a far more adventurous traveler. Now she makes a special effort to tone it down. I am grateful for small favors. I don't think I could have survived an un-toned-down Nancy. I cannot under any circumstances see myself trekking through the mountains of Nepal, or across the Torres del Paine (well named, I should think) in Patagonia, or on a 12-day horseback ride in Wyoming looking for the source of Lake Yellowstone. These are the kinds of things Nancy did when she was single.

In short we have accommodated, fitting one to the other the way couples do when they spoon in bed. Nancy is Africa. I am South America. I have learned to shape myself to her contours. She has learned to soften them.

But that's about as far as I can go. Travel will never be an unqualified good for me. I don't think I will ever shake my underlying anxiety of living in a dangerous world, no matter how well I understand it. It is an old tape that is simply inerasable. Come to think of it, it has been with me my entire life, ever since that first memory of being locked in a bathroom not because of anything I did, but because of the way the world is. I shut the door. The hook came to life and found its eyelet. As far as that hook was concerned, I was so much Muzak. I believe we are born with dispositions. Mine was to see the world into which I was thrust as a hostile place. I don't think it was an accident that the bathroom incident was my earliest memory. That memory reinforced my disposition and, come to think of it, vice versa.

The best I can do is recognize it for what it is, have another martini (vodka) and hope the trip will end without incident. As I write this, I am listening to early 16th century madrigals. The fact is I can't work without noise. That's what it is like when I travel. My background music is anxiety. It is always there. And even though I may be going through the most interesting place in the world—say, the Pyramid of Cheops— that background noise is saying something like, "Suppose one of these stones comes loose and blocks the way out. What will you do then?"

As I come to the end of this book, I am put in mind of coming to the end of a trip with Nancy. For both of us the hardest part is the last hour. That is when we have packed, left our room or our tent, and carried our luggage to a central location, a lobby, or the dining tent of our campsite, waiting for our baggage to be loaded onto the van that will take us on the first leg of our voyage home. It is hard for me because it is sheer hell on Nancy. She knows that it is all about to end. She doesn't want that to happen. So she calculates what she can possibly do in the little time that's left.

On the 9th of July, 2000, we were waiting for the van to pick us up at the Victoria Falls Hotel in Zimbabwe. It would be there in less than an hour. Suddenly, Nancy jumped up, gathered her cameras and before I could object, ran out of the hotel and down the path toward the falls.

"I'll be right back," she yelled over her shoulder. "Turn on the walkie-talkie."

I rummaged through our luggage. I found the walkie-talkie and called her.

"Where the hell are you?" I pleaded. "The van will be here in half an hour."

She had gone back to the falls for one last view, one last picture. She was like a drunk at closing time, ordering that one last drink.

"There are about 30 baboons on the path in front of me," she said in a tone of voice half excitement and half a terrible sadness.

"Male baboons can be very hostile to women," I warned. "You could be in danger. Turn around."

The walkie-talkie went dead.

"Nancy, are you there? Nancy, answer me."

Nothing.

"That's it," I said to myself. "I'm going down there."

And I would have, too. Only I saw her bouncing back up the path, holding the camera in triumph over her head.

"Boy, did I get some great shots of a baboon," she said.

I will continue to travel with Nancy as long as she lives. If she dies before me, then I will make one last trip, the one I promised her I would make—scattering a bit of her ashes on every continent on the face of the earth. If I die before her, our backyard patio will do.

Here's hoping I go first.

ACKNOWLEDGMENTS

There are a great many people to thank for this book if, indeed, "thank" is the right word. ("Blame" might be closer to the mark.) Whichever it is, certainly at the top of the list has to be Melissa Chapman Gresh and Heather Garcia of the MIT Alumni Travel Program. They made many of the trips described in this book possible. Without their good offices this book would never have happened.

Equally important to the writing of this book are George and Gaby Whitehouse, proprietors of *Custom African Travel Services* (CATS), the engine that drove a great many of the trips described here. Grudgingly, I have to admit that their consummate knowledge of the travel business has not led to a single misstep.

Thanks also to the indefatigable women of the Women's Travel Club, of which my wife, is president. They have listened to my complaints with the understanding of nuns in a nunnery and then gone on to tell me about their own travel adventures that, not to put too fine a point on it, dwarf mine the way an 18-wheeler dwarfs a four-wheel *Radio Flyer*.

Some of these intrepid club members I have actually traveled with. Kathryn Willmore and her sister, Dena, top the list of brave souls whose gusto for travel rivals a lion's for red meat. I will never forget the day they strode alone into the center of the village at Victoria Falls. As I watched them disappear around a bend in the road, I felt as if I were saying goodbye to Lewis and Clark.

Then there are the by now hundreds of people I have traveled with who listened to passages from my journals while we were together and whose sympathetic responses encouraged me to go on writing. Wherever you are, thank you for listening.

Another group willing to listen with patience and even on occasion approval is the Moses Seminar at MIT. Named after its convener, Joel Moses, its members are a faithful and kindly lot who have smiled, sometimes indulgently, at several of the incidents in this book. I thank them for their gentle and steadfast support.

Certain individuals have also stepped forward to sympathize with and support me in my travel neurosis. Emily Heistand is one. She set aside space on the web page of MIT's School of Humanities, Arts, and Social Sciences for my journals, my readings, and for Nancy Kelly's photographs (http://shass.mit.edu/news/reluctant-traveler). I am grateful to her.

Maggy Bruzelius has also aided and abetted me in sharing my pain with a wider community. I am in her debt as well.

The photograph of the author asleep on the cover is the candid work of Barbara "Boo" Price, who has managed to put into a single picture the thousands of words I have put into this book. Sitting next to me is my wife, Nancy. Behind me is Kathryn Willmore and next to her Terry Eastman, all intrepid travelers. Thanks to Boo, also, for the photograph of the author on an elephant and at the Equator at the end of this book.

Boo is also responsible for a priceless video of Ugandan children singing "I am the youngest star" under the direction of one of the best African guides anyone has ever encountered, Cliff Kisitu. His story is told in Chapter 8. The reader who is moved by it might want to see Boo's video on the Internet. Search for "The Reluctant Traveler Keyser." Then, in the blog's search box, search for "youngest star."

Thanks to my long-time friend and assistant, Charlotte Gibbs, a marvelous painter in her own right, who listened sympathetically, helped me with many issues of design and insisted that I compensate her by taking her lunch.

Thanks to Barbara Wallraff, a portion of Chapter 5, *The Lion Torture*, appeared in the May 2000 issue of *The Atlantic Monthly* under the title "Faint of Heart in the Heart of Darkness." Since then Barbara, Nancy and I have gone on to become close friends much to my good fortune. She has read earlier versions of the ms., and has provided me with the invaluable advice and support that only a real professional can offer. I am in her immense debt.

Thanks also to Nancy Kelly for the extremely friendly portrait on the back cover.

A number of others have given me their support as well by reading and endorsing earlier versions of the manuscript, among them Naomi Chase, Jean Flanagan, Morris Halle, and Mariève Rugo. Their unflagging encouragement has been a godsend.

The lion's share of the gratitude carcass must go to Deborah Chasman. She took a rambling ms. and turned it into a coherent one by whatever magic it is that she has at her fingertips. It was quite a trick. Without Deborah there would be no book.

A heartfelt thank-you goes to my son, Benjamin, for his support of the book and of me. A special thank-you I reserve for my daughter, Beth, who read earlier versions and whose constant cheerleading on behalf of my writing meant more to me than she will ever know.

And really finally, my thanks and my love belong to my

Jay and Nancy at a moon gate in the wall surrounding Xidi, a 15th century merchant village in Anhui Province, after the rain has stopped. They still have rain booties on.

wife, Nancy Kelly. Her photographs grace this book, an infinitesimal sample of her creativity, as the reader will soon discover. Her addiction to photography and to travel made me an enabler and all the richer for it. Talk about win-win situations.

Samuel Jay Keyser
Cambridge, MA
May 28, 2011

Cliff Kisitu, Jay Keyser, Ben Musisi
The Equator, Uganda
March 5, 2007

ABOUT THE AUTHOR

SAMUEL JAY KEYSER is Professor Emeritus of Linguistics at the Massachusetts Institute of Technology and editor of the journal *Linguistic Inquiry* and of the *Linguistic Inquiry Monograph Series*. In addition to writing many scholarly works, he is the author of a book of poems, *Raising the Dead* (Garden Street Press, 1993). His book of children's poems, *The Pond God and Other Stories* (Front Street Books, 2003), won the *Lee Bennett Hopkins Poetry Honor Award* in 2004. Dr. Keyser plays trombone with *Aardvark*, an avant garde jazz orchestra, and with *The New Liberty Jazz Band*, a Dixieland band in the New Orleans tradition.

He resides in Cambridge, Massachusetts, where he hopes against hope that Nancy's next trip will be cancelled.